ROUGH CUT MEN

DAVID DUSEK

Made for Success
PUBLISHING

Made For Success Publishing
P.O. Box 1775 Issaquah, WA 98027
www.MadeForSuccessPublishing.com

Unless otherwise indicated, all Scripture is taken from the HOLY BIBLE, NEW INTERNATIONAL VERSION™. Copyright © 1973, 1978, 1984 by International Bible Society. Used by permission of Zondervan. All rights reserved.

Additional Scripture is taken from the Holy Bible, New Living Translation, Copyright © 1996, 2004, 2007. Used by permission of Tyndale House Publishers, Inc., Wheaton, Illinois 60189. All rights reserved.

Distributed by Made For Success Publishing

Library of Congress Cataloging-in-Publication data Dusek, David
Rough Cut Men: A Man's Battle Guide to Building Real Relationships with Each Other, and with Jesus
p. cm.
ISBN: 978-1-61339-786-2
LCCN: 2015903482

1. Religion / Christian Life / Men's Issues
2. Religion / Christian Life / Personal Growth
3. Religion / Christian Life / Relationships
4. Religion / Christian Ministry / Discipleship

Printed in the United States of America

For further information contact Made for Success Publishing, +1 425 526 6480 or email at Service@madeforsuccess.net

This book is dedicated to my amazing wife, Joni. For all the countless times I have been ready to give up on ministry and you refused to let me, thank you. For the way you love me, thank you. And for the way you reflect the face of Christ in our marriage, thank you. I love you very much.

Contents

Introduction

Right out of the gate, I want to give you a word of caution. I am not a theologian or a Bible scholar, nor am I a retired professional athlete or decorated soldier. I am just a regular guy trying to make it through life while the world attempts to derail me every day. I go to church; work 80 hours per week; and have five teenagers, two college tuitions, and a wonderful wife. And yeah, not a day goes by where I don't feel like sitting down on my couch to watch 24 hours of ESPN SportsCenter.

And every time I feel like I have it all under control, the wheels come flying off my life again. Can you feel me?

Through divorce, remarriage, death, suicide attempts, loss, and major career changes, two things have been a consistent and driving force in my life.

The first pillar is the man known as Jesus Christ. He has never walked away from me, nor will He. And in spite of me, He continues to love me, bless me, and walk with me through seemingly unbeatable odds. You are going to read a lot about Him in these pages.

The second anchor in my life is my friend, David. He has been my covering fire, my support, my coach and even the guy who tells me I am being an idiot when I get off-track. You are also going to hear a lot about this guy as we roll through *Rough Cut Men*

Those two guys I just mentioned are actually the reason for *Rough Cut Men*. God has given me a laser-focused vision: to get men to engage with other guys and with Jesus Christ.

Let me tell you that this book is not another men's ministry how-to guide or a handbook to tell you how to live your life like me. The book in your hands is full of "guy movie" references, stories of men in the world who you most likely know, some personal testimony, and a good dose of biblical truth. And by the time you hit the last page, my prayer is that you have a friend, a Jonathan, with whom you can walk through life.

The single mission of this book is to create friendships. Read it with a few guys then meet up and hit the discussion questions hard. At the end of each chapter you will find discussion questions called **ACTIVATION QUESTIONS**. In military jargon "activation" is defined as the "order to active duty." In other words, training is over and it's time to go to war.

The resulting friendships that are formed will be nothing short of astounding, as I have conducted the live event hundreds of times with similar results.

So, after conducting live *Rough Cut Men* events for years, I realized it was time to put this all down on paper. So hang on, bro....

THERE AIN'T NO SUCH THING TODAY, BOY

O kay, I admit it. I am a war history buff. It really doesn't matter if the weapon is a musket, a sword, or a Howitzer—I am all over it. And it frankly doesn't matter too much which war either. Now throw in my penchant for action movies and I become every wife's worst nightmare. I bet I could sit and watch *Saving Private Ryan* end to end for a week and never get sick of it.

One of the best war movies ever? *We Were Soldiers*, hands down. This is a true story adapted from a book by the same name, written by two guys who were right there in the middle of the battle. And not just any two guys, but the commanding officer, Lt. Col. Hal Moore and UPI correspondent Joe Galloway, who was assigned to cover the first push of US soldiers into Vietnam. Add Mel Gibson, Sam Elliott, and Barry Pepper (aka, "Jackson" the sniper from *Saving Private Ryan*) and you have the best war movie in the English-speaking world.

Moore, played by Mel Gibson, is in command of the 450-man 1st Battalion of the 7th Cavalry, which is dropped via helicopter onto a small patch of ground tagged as "LZ X-Ray" in the Ia Drang Valley of Vietnam on November 14, 1965. Col. Moore, along with Sgt. Maj. Basil Plumley, portrayed by Sam Elliott, and the whole Battalion come head-to-head with more than 2,000 North Vietnamese. And because of the new era of television, the UPI also sends in war correspondent Joe Galloway (Barry Pepper) to capture the whole "dominating US operation" on film for the nation to see firsthand at the dinner table. Yep, it's a recipe for a disaster.

Within hours, an entire platoon is lost, the helicopters are taking more bodies out of LZ X-Ray than they are bringing in, and the Vietnamese are popping out of little holes in the mountain like angry fire ants from every direction. The 7th Cavalry is trying to kill them while Joe Galloway is attempting to take compelling pictures. Then it becomes clear the US ground forces are about to get overrun.

The subsequent movie scene always gets me. It reminds me of a lot of guys, myself included. Joe Galloway officially curls up on the ground in the fetal position in the hopes of not getting killed, which isn't looking too good at this point. Plumley, using his best Sam Elliott deep-voiced impersonation, says, "You can't take any pictures from down there, sonny." As Galloway pops back up, Plumley hands him a rifle. Galloway's reply? "I'm a non-combatant, sir." You've got to love Plumley's reaction to Galloway: "There ain't no such thing today."

Have you ever felt pinned down by the gunfire of life, afraid to poke your head up out of the foxhole? Junk just keeps crawling out of holes at you like those Vietnamese soldiers? I know I have. But men, we need to see it for what it really is.

Jesus gives us a very lucid visual description of what we are up against:

The thief comes only to steal, kill and destroy.

John 10:10

Properly translated from the original Greek text, the words "steal," "kill," and "destroy" mean "steal," "kill," and "destroy."

When we get up every morning, we have a very real enemy who really wants us out of the picture. If he takes us down, he takes our families down with us. Even if you are on your spiritual "A game," the enemy will come after your wife or your kids to try and take you out.

Gentlemen, we are at war. It's time to quit lying on the ground, get up, claim the victory that is ours through Jesus Christ, and start squeezing off rounds. There ain't no such thing as a non-combatant. Not today or any day.

Let's go to war together!

Activation Questions

- *Has there been a time in my life when I have felt completely pinned down and facing incredible odds?*

- *How did I respond?*

2.

"SAFE" IS OVERRATED
(Becoming a Dangerous Man)

One word used to come to mind when I thought of any kind of auto racing: "boring." Watching a bunch of cars drive around a circle on TV? Oddly enough, I would watch bowling or golf, but racing? Just not my thing.

That all changed when I became a part of an Indy Car pit crew in 1992 (they were called CART cars back then, for you open wheel purists). I lived in Portland, Oregon at the time and a local racing team was attempting to put together the first "all-athlete" pit crew by soliciting recruits from local gyms. I was a gym rat in my 20s, and somehow they managed to pique my interest enough to try out. Up until this point, the average pit crew consisted of the guys who could at least make it over the wall. The athlete concept was new, the brainchild of a guy who worked at Nike.

If you know much about racing in the new millennium, virtually every pit crew these days is comprised entirely of athletes. When it comes to mechanical aptitude, many pit men don't know much more about the inner workings of the cars than the drivers do. These guys are professional athletes, trained by the likes of Lance Armstrong's personal trainer at on-site gyms that rival any NFL team. With millions of sponsorship dollars involved, racing is now a big-ticket business. And since every second spent in the pits represents an entire football field on the race track, race shops invest a ton of money in their "over the wall" crew.

Well, out of 88 guys who tried out, I made the top nine. The only problem was that the team only needed eight guys, so I was out. I had "fumbled" a rear tire during a relay and fell face-down into a concrete floor, but I got back up in spite of the blood to finish the relay. Fortunately for me, due to the intense training and practice schedule, one of the men ahead of me dropped out. Evidently my bloody second effort in the relay caught the eye of the team owners, so I spent most of May 1992 in Speedway, Indiana. I learned to love racing and the guys on my team, and it was a bitter pill to swallow when our car failed to qualify; the team went bankrupt and we all went home. My new career in motorsports was over before it started. But my passion for racing was birthed that year.

Since then, I answered the call into ministry and have spoken at the NASCAR Sprint Cup shop of Joe Gibbs Racing several times. I love the culture and racing in general. Deep down, every guy wants to belong to a successful effort, focusing on something greater than themselves, and racing is definitely a team sport.

Now you may or may not be a race fan. In my travels, I have discovered a lot of guys who either love it or hate it. There isn't much gray, so to speak. And when you poll male race fans, which I have only done in a very unscientific fashion (aka, by asking them), what do you suppose is the principal overwhelming draw toward racing? Let me ask the question another way: What are guys waiting for when they watch a race?

The crashes. The "big one." They want twisted metal and con-crete, fire and smoke… with no driver injuries, of course. We want to see half of the 43-car field crash with five laps to go.

But times have changed in the world of motorsports, gentle-men.

Last year, my son Jordan and I spent some time in Day-tona during "Speed Week." Traditionally, the Thursday before the Daytona 500 consists of a lot of practice laps and two sepa-rate qualifying races. And if you are a NASCAR fan at all, you may have noticed that they keep modifying the cars. They look different, sound different, and frankly look more like a regular "daily driver" than ever.

As a bit of racing background, you non-race fans should know a few historical facts about stock car racing. First, at the in-ception of stock car racing, the cars themselves were essentially the same models you could buy off the showroom floor, with much bigger motors and a number spray painted on the door. They drove on sand and dirt, for crying out loud. The cars had four-point seatbelts, metal dashboards, and drivers who wore nothing more than shop overalls and an open-faced helmet. And if they were really lucky, they had a fire extinguisher on board.

In addition, even when they finally moved to real race tracks instead of the beach, the walls were solid concrete and speeds increased to a shade more than 200 MPH. And the guy with the checkered flag stood ON the track when the winner flew by. Racing was, by all counts, the definition of danger.

At breakfast before our time at the track, I read an interesting article in a national newspaper that had opted to run a series of

NASCAR articles in the week leading up to the race. This particular article was all about safety. It really struck me as an oxymoron, but the article served as a parable of sorts on why guys are avoiding both churches and relationships like the plague.

In no particular order, the writer pointed out that the "Car of Tomorrow" (the new, smaller version of the typical Cup car) is equipped with crumple zones, collapsible steering wheels, 10-point roll cages, and all kinds of safety features. The cars have smaller restrictor plates that limit the flow of fuel into the carburetors and consequently slow them down. The new walls at the speedway are now called SAFER barriers and were comprised of something like the old Styrofoam coolers we used to fill with ice and beer. The walls around the track essentially collapse and absorb the impact of a crash. Additionally, due to the untimely death of Dale Earnhardt, every car now has head and neck restraint systems to avoid injury and all drivers MUST wear full-face helmets. Man, these days even the pit crew wears fire suits and helmets to change a tire!

The article culminated with an interesting statistic: NASCAR was losing the male fan demographic between the ages of 18-26. Really? Imagine that. Guys in that age group are watching UFC and the X Games, where athletes take skateboards down 90-degree ramps with nothing more than a brain bucket on their head. The last thing a young man wants to see is something touted as "safe." And in their effort to slow down a sport based on speed and soften a sport where crashes are an integral part of the experience, NASCAR is losing a very large part of their fan base.

Guess what? It isn't any different in the church. We have turned church into a place to go, not a Person to follow. We have created flowery, happy places where everyone appears to be an inch deep and a mile wide. We have slowed it down, dumbed it down, and frankly made the church experience so archaic that it's really no wonder the younger generations as a whole are finding other ways to spend their time. While we admit we need a Savior, we have packaged the "church experience" in a pretty white robe. Understand that I am a huge proponent of the organized church and believe that every believer needs to be connected to the body through a home church, but it's almost as if the Stepford family has moved in. Church is safe, quiet, and completely uncompelling to most men, especially the young guys.

Make no mistake. Jesus was a man's man. God chose very specifically to come down to earth and blend in. He was a blue-collar worker, a carpenter. If you have ever worked with wood, you know that splinters and calluses come with the job. And while He was perfect and fully God and fully man, I often wonder if Jesus didn't at least occasionally bash his thumb with a hammer.

Jesus also entered the temple courts and was furious when he saw a mini-mall set up in His temple:

> *Jesus entered the temple area and drove out all who were buying and selling there. He overturned the tables of the money changers and the benches of those selling doves. "It is written," he said to them, " 'My house will be called a house of prayer,' but you are making it a 'den of robbers.' "*
>
> *Matthew 21:12-13*

Notice that Jesus didn't start the sentence with "If it isn't too much trouble…"? He was righteously indignant, backed it up with His own Word, and tossed everybody out on their tails. Does that sound warm and fuzzy to you?

It is high time men resume their rightful positions as spiritual leaders in the home, community, marketplace, and the church. It begins and ends with us, gentlemen. We don't need a comfortable pew or a cup of coffee and a hymnal. After all, Jesus didn't even have a place to live:

> *Jesus replied, "Foxes have holes and birds of the air have nests, but the Son of Man has no place to lay his head."*
>
> *Luke 9:58*

And following Jesus Christ was never intended to be safe or boring, was it? Taking up the cross isn't easy. It's big, heavy, and hard to move—and it takes a real guy to carry one.

So let's recap:

1. Jesus was a man's man, not a watered down wimp. It's time to reclaim the masculinity that embodies the very Person we follow.

2. Following Jesus was never intended to be safe or comfortable. The cross is heavy and it takes a strong man to carry it. Denying ourselves requires sacrifice. Period.

3. We have to determine what we want the church to look like and create an environment that will draw in thrill-seekers. Lord knows we have enough "pew-sitting bless-me sponges" in the grandstands watching.

There's a reason why the Bible is called the "sword of the Spirit" (Eph. 6:17). The last time I looked, the sword was an offensive weapon designed for attack. How much more unsafe can you get than a sword? It's a weapon of war. God wants His warriors back and it's time to pick up a weapon.

Activation Questions

- *Am I connected to a local church?*

- *If not, what caused me to disengage?*

- *What would it take to get me back in the battle and connected?*

3.

FROM MUSKETS TO MISSILES
(The Warfare Has Changed)

Over the past few years, I have stood on some pretty amazing battlefields, ranging from the Revolutionary War to the Civil War. While I have never seen any combat personally, I know a lot of men who fought for our country in Vietnam, Desert Storm, and even World War II. One thing that fascinates me is how war has changed in just more than a few hundred years.

Back in the days of the Revolution, men lined up in ranks and marched head to head onto the battlefield. There were two ranks of men each, both walking toward one another until they were in range of their horribly inaccurate muskets. Once the two armies were within firing distance, the front rank would drop to one knee and the back rank would literally line their musket barrels up in between the heads of the guys in front of them. Then came a volley of musket balls in both directions. Basically, whoever fired the most musket balls would win.

The British were defeated in large part due to a type of combat that they had not experienced in previous theaters. The Continental Army had militiamen firing from behind trees, out of haylofts, and from dozens of hidden locations. Today, we call this "guerrilla warfare." The element of surprise, coupled with the unparalleled tenacity of a bunch of farmers-turned-soldiers, sent the British home and gained independence for a new nation.

The Civil War was a total aberration, as the weapons were still pretty primitive and the men killing each other were brothers, relatives, or friends. As to whether you fought as a Confederate soldier or a Union soldier, it all depended upon the side of the line on which you were born. And to quote Forrest Gump, "That's all I have to say about that."

Then we progressed into the more conventional warfare of the World War era. Planes, paratroopers, and tanks were introduced. We could attack from the ground, the sea, or the air at any point, and the technology was radically advanced. We had the ability to fire weapons from much greater distances and far more accurately. And of course, with the help of some nuclear scientists, we developed a weapon that could destroy entire cities and bring conflicts to a swift and decisive end. Suffice it to say, during this era there wasn't an army in the world that could stand up to ours.

Then came Vietnam. In the opening chapter, you read about our nation's initiation into this conflict, which spanned a decade and resulted in almost 60,000 killed in action. We marched into Vietnam, confident (probably much too confident) that our superior weaponry would easily outmatch the North Vietnamese Army. The US Army had no contingency plan to combat an enemy that utilized civilian children as human shields, employed the use of hidden tripwires, or covered pits full of sharpened sticks. And the same guerilla warfare that the Continental Army used so successfully to defeat the British came back to bite us almost two hundred years later.

Not to belabor the whole war topic, but when we entered the desert combat era in the early 1990s, I recall an issue with tanks that wouldn't run in the sand. Oops. And if memory serves, our first detachments deployed into desert warfare donned green camouflage. Green? It's sort of hard to hide when you look like the only tree on the beach. I have heard it said, "If you can be seen, you can be hit. If you can be hit, you can be killed." Needless to say, we made some corrections to both the tanks and the uniforms. But all of the best weapons and soldiers in the world don't help you find dudes hiding in little caves, which has been the latest tactic used by the enemy.

My point in this brief and hopefully somewhat accurate recap of some of our major war efforts as a "new" nation is to illustrate one very important fact:

WARFARE CHANGES

One of the craziest statistics I have ever read referred to Basic Training, which is essentially learning the "ins and outs" of being a combat-ready soldier. At the onset of our involvement in WWII, Basic Training lasted roughly 12 weeks, with some form of advanced training to follow. Ultimately, the total time invested in training a soldier ranged from 15 to 22 weeks, dependent upon his job.

By the end of the Vietnam War, Basic Training was shaved down to about eight weeks. Although the type of combat was like nothing ever experienced in prior wars, the training was significantly shorter. Much of the training for Vietnam was likely "trial by fire," as our losses mounted quickly and we needed boots on the ground in the jungle.

You know what? ***SPIRITUAL WARFARE CHANGES, TOO!*** And just like Vietnam, a lot of guys these days are learning warfare in the same "trial by fire" theater. With the inception of the Internet and social media, we are fast discovering just how far off of the mark we men are. And it appears that, as a church (the people, not the building), we are more reactive than we are proactive. Times have changed and we need to catch up.

The apostle Paul, in his letter to the church in Ephesus, gives us a vivid illustration of spiritual warfare. And it withstands the test of time, irrespective of the era:

> *For our struggle is not against flesh and blood, but against the rulers, against the authorities, against the powers of this dark world and against the spiritual forces of evil in the heavenly realms.*
>
> *Ephesians 6:12*

We aren't battling the guy next door, or the government, or our bosses. And we aren't engaged with just any enemy but with rulers, authorities, and powers. We aren't dealing with the enlisted guys in Satan's army but the commissioned officers with the field training designed to kick our butts without proper training. It's interesting to note you won't find these dark spiritual forces hiding in your closet or under your bed but "in heavenly realms." The King James Version refers to it as "in high places." It's easy to breeze right past Ephesians 6:12 and miss some of those key points. We are battling some bad dudes and that battle is raging on over our heads.

To illustrate the concept of "heavenly realms," look at Job. In the very first chapter, God literally gives permission to Satan to mess with one of His favorite children. God gives the enemy, who's hoping that Job will curse God at some point, free reign to upend Job's entire life. Enter Satan:

> *One day the angels came to present themselves before the Lord, and Satan also came with them. The Lord said to Satan, "Where have you come from?"*

> *Job 1:6*

Please note that God and Satan didn't run into each other at a bus stop or an angel convention. Satan and one of his flunkies barged into God's office! And in that "high place" Paul was talking about! In a way, it almost seems like God is stunned by Satan's boldness in just walking in.

I swear, sometimes I think Satan just sits right outside of God's office with a glass up to the door hoping to thwart yet another one of God's plans in our lives. Have you ever noticed that when you pray for something very specific, there is often an equal but not so fun counterattack to the prayer? A coincidence? I think not.

While the location of the initial battle hasn't changed since the time of Job, the methods used by the enemy have certainly changed. Twenty years ago, if a man wanted to see a pornographic movie, he would have to park his car behind a rundown theater, hoping his neighbor wouldn't see his car. Today, the Internet is streaming right into our living rooms and our smart phones. A man can close the door and scroll away without anyone seeing or knowing. Instead of fighting the enemy on the battlefield, we are letting him right into our homes and into our pockets.

Social media sites have become a staple in our society as well. With the likes of Facebook and Twitter, we are now connected to friends we knew in high school. People we haven't seen, and in some cases didn't really ever want to see again, are finding us online.

I'm certainly not advocating abandoning the Internet because of this. In point of fact, unchurched men are using the Internet to attend virtual services online. Longtime church guys are opting for online church as opposed to getting up and driving to brick and mortar buildings. And the traditional paper Bibles have been jettisoned by many guys, who have opted to use Bible applications like YouVersion to get into the Word.

As with any tool or weapon, the Internet can be a benefit or a detriment, depending on how one uses it. It's like gasoline. If you fill your car with gasoline, it will run and get you where you need to be. But if you pull up to a gas station, jump out of your car, douse yourself with unleaded and strike a match, you are going to burn up. Same gasoline, different application.

Satan has found a crack in the door, and he is killing us through our use, or misuse, of the Internet. One way to battle an Internet integrity issue is through the use of Internet filters and accountability tools. These tracking programs will alert a self-designated accountability partner when someone goes down the wrong path.

Now I don't want to dwell on the Internet or pornography, but since it affects more than 50% of the men in church (that's a 2006 statistic, so you can imagine it's likely a lot higher now), it's worth revisiting. That's half of the men in the church. Half.

Did you know that Paul hit on this topic as well, in a letter to the church in Corinth? He simply writes:

Flee from sexual immorality

1 Corinthians 6:18

"Flee" means "run." Not trot, but run like you are on fire. Get away from it. In other words, don't try to face it, but run from it. Why? Because sexual immorality, or in our case, Internet pornography, is a tough battle to face. Especially alone.

Earlier, we read what Paul had to say about spiritual battles in Ephesians 6. This chapter is really his warfare chapter, because not only does Paul address the type of enemy we are facing, but he also tells us what gear to bring to the fight:

Therefore put on the full armor of God, so that when the day of evil comes, you may be able to stand your ground, and after you have done everything, to stand. Stand firm then, with the belt of truth buckled around your waist, with the breastplate of righteousness in place, and with your feet fitted with the readiness that comes from the gospel of peace. In addition to all this, take up the shield of faith, with which you can extinguish all the flaming arrows of the evil one. Take the helmet of salvation and the sword of the Spirit, which is the word of God.

Ephesians 6:13-17

Armor, a helmet, a sword, proper footwear, and a shield. That's heavy stuff for a serious war. So if the armor of God is designed to go toe-to-toe with the powers and principalities of evil, then why does Paul tell us to run away from sexual immorality?

To answer that question, you need an image of a soldier's armor circa the life of Paul. First century armor was comprised of leather, sheet metal, rivets, and straps. The shields and swords were obviously metal, as was the helmet. The breastplate was attached to the front of the torso and was typically secured in the back with straps, as were the leg protectors. The shield was carried out front, as was the sword. Do you have a visual now? What's missing?

If you happened to notice there was nothing on the back of the torso or legs, you are correct. Most light infantry armor had nothing but straps on the back. If you were a soldier in this era, you didn't really need armor on your back, as you engaged the enemy face-to-face, toe-to-toe.

So while the armor Paul alludes to is more than adequate for spiritual battle, the armor is just not quite strong enough to battle sexual immorality head on. Basically, it's easier to flee and live to fight another day. But here's the catch. If the armor only covers the front, and a soldier opts to flee, isn't his backside wide open to attack? After all, there isn't any armor back there, remember?

The only way for a soldier to successfully flee from sexually immorality is to have another man behind him, facing backward, to deflect the arrows. The only way to survive the spiritual warfare of the 21st Century is back to back. Spiritual warfare has indeed changed, and we need to upgrade our battle preparedness in order to defend our homes, our children, and our marriages.

Activation Questions

- *Is there a particular battle that I feel, or have felt, ill-prepared to deal with?*

- *What can I do differently as I train for this new affront, both spiritually and practically? In other words, how can I beat it?*

- *Who can I connect with in my area to properly equip me for this type of battle?*

4.
BACK TO BACK
(Every Man's Need for Support)

Any man who has ever been in a combat theater, or served in law enforcement, will tell you that there are a few non-negotiable "must-haves" to do the job. The first is obviously the right tools, like a weapon, body armor and, of course, better aim than the other guy. The second revolves around other men. Every man in a heavy combat arena needs covering fire—someone who has their back. In battle, a soldier will never wander off into the jungle or the desert without another man scanning the horizon for the enemy. Any good soldier just assumes there is a sniper in the trees waiting to pick him off, so the inherent response to that is to always be prepared to take out the sniper trained to kill you.

Life is no different in the theater in which most of us men find ourselves every day. We are on a mission to provide for our family, live pure lives, and be the best men we can be for God. But off in the trees, fully prepared to squeeze a round off at us, is a very real enemy who would like nothing better than to see us fail at that mission. Yet, by and large, we roll out of bed and into the world without a shred of body armor or covering fire. And not only that, but we also desperately need other men to encourage us when we are beaten down, to be our emotional dumping ground when we need it and to tell us we are being an idiot when we get off track. *Every man needs support, encouragement and accountability.* Don't worry. I'm going to unpack all three purposes of other men in our lives in the next few chapters.

Do you remember the movie *Forrest Gump*? It's the story of a special needs man who, for some unknown reason, accomplishes some pretty amazing stuff. Among other things, he plays football for the University of Alabama (this pains me as a diehard Florida Gator fan), meets several presidents, builds a flourishing business, and is a world-class ping pong player. Tom Hanks, by the way, is perhaps one of the most talented actors to ever pick up a script. Think about *Saving Private Ryan*, *Big*, or *Philadelphia* if you need proof. Do yourself a favor, though, and just ignore the whole *Bosom Buddies* thing.

I don't want to focus our attention on Forrest, but rather I want to look at his "best good friend," Benjamin Buford Blue, more commonly known as "Bubba." If you've seen the movie, one word probably pops into your head when I mention the name Bubba. "Shrimp." Coconut shrimp, boiled shrimp, shrimp scampi, shrimp sandwich… and the list goes on. Bubba is a simple guy from Bayou La Batre, Alabama, and he comes from a long line of shrimpers. Shrimp are this guy's passion.

The relationship between Forrest and Bubba is brief. They meet each other on a bus on the way to boot camp, shortly after Forrest graduates from Alabama. The Vietnam War is in full swing, and both men find themselves headed to Southeast Asia. You may recall that only two people ever permitted Forrest to sit beside them on a bus. One was Jenny, his lifelong girlfriend of sorts, and the other was Bubba. The two men instantly become friends, and as their friendship grows, Bubba extends Forrest the opportunity to go into the "shrimpin' bitness" with him, which Forrest gladly accepts. Unfortunately, their friendship is cut short when Bubba is killed in an ambush.

There is a scene in *Forrest Gump* that illustrates how we could potentially revolutionize the way we relate to other men if we truly wrap our minds around the concept. You see, most of us men today have hundreds of acquaintances and absolutely no friends. We can rattle off names of the men who go to our church and work right beside us, but we know nothing about them. It's easy to remember names, especially if the guys are wearing name tags, but trying to tear down the walls we have built up around ourselves is a much more daunting task.

The scene in question encompasses exactly 36 seconds of the film, but the words uttered by Army PFC Benjamin Blue are profound. It's the middle of the night in the jungles of Vietnam and the rain is unrelenting. Our two friends are on watch, scanning the horizon for the enemy and Bubba simply says, "Hey Forrest. You lean back against me and I'll lean right back against you. That way, we don't have to fall asleep with our heads in the mud. You know why we a good partnership, Forrest? 'Cuz we be watchin' out for one another, likes brothers and stuff."

Brilliant! You lean back against me, and I'll lean back against you. That way, we don't end up face-down in the swamp. Did you know that there is only one way two men can cover a 360-degree perimeter? Back-to-back. If you are in a flanking position, your backside is still compromised. If you are shoulder-to-shoulder, you can still get dropped from the rear. When two men are back-to-back, there is a commitment that no one will approach from my 180-degree horizon and no one will get to us from yours.

One other advantage to being back to back is a simple matter of gravity. The full weight of one man will offset the weight of the other. Two guys can sit that way, without a tree stump or secondary support, all night long. Bubba caps the statement by likening their relationship to being brothers, which essentially paraphrases Proverbs 17:17:

A friend loves at all times, but a brother is born for adversity

Proverbs 17:17

Like you, I have had my fair share of "adversity" in my life. And through it all, I have had one friend who has been right there in the muddy jungle with me. His name is David. This guy executes his role in my life near perfectly, being my support, my encourager and, of course, the guy who sets me straight when I need it.

I am one of the 42% of the men you will meet, serving in the church, who are divorced and remarried. I make no apologies for it since that divorce is what led me to the Lord. I prefer to call it a "head-on collision with the cross," since that's what it felt like, but the end result was the same. Along with salvation came the heavy price of my losing almost everything, including my two very young children. And because I had met my ex-wife in the Pacific Northwest, and I didn't want to "rock the boat," I gave her permission to move back to Seattle with my children.

My introduction to God Himself occurred at the top of the Sunshine Skyway Bridge, which spans Tampa Bay from

St. Petersburg to Bradenton. It is 174 feet from the driving deck to the water, and because of this, the bridge has been the site of more than 130 suicides. And every few feet at the precipice, you will find red crisis intervention phones. No, I wasn't a jumper. I was driving over that bridge, and upon realizing I was closer to this "God" who I didn't really know, I cried out, "God, if You're there, I need to know it!" Every hair on my arms stood up, and I knew God was there. Within weeks, I was baptized, and within years, I was in full-time ministry. I am a true Saul-to-Paul convert in every sense of the word.

So there I sat in Florida, with my two kids now 4,000 miles and three time zones away. They did spend the summer with me, with the inevitable return flight always looming on the horizon. I recall a summer of Disney trips, the beach, and miniature golf which, after four weeks, culminated with me watching their airplane become a small dot in the sky while sobbing like a little girl. I remember being despondent as I drove past landmark after landmark that reminded me of their visit. And I can still hear my ex-wife's words, "I hate Florida. If you ever want to see your kids for more than a summer, you will have to move to Seattle."

Then, five days of depression later, my then-fiancé Joni (who, by the way, is living proof that God exists) called me on the phone, insisting we pray. I don't know if you've ever had one of those times when the last thing you felt like doing was praying, but this was one of those times for me. You know what I mean? "Hey, we need to pray about this," they say. "Knock yourself out," you think to yourself, "but don't expect any participation out of me. I'm done!"

While Joni prayed, I just listened. She asked God to bring my kids back to Florida for good. Now I'm thinking, "Really?

My ex hates me and hates Florida. No chance." Well, within a day, my ex-wife called and said, "The kids need to be near you. We're moving back to Florida." Lessons learned? First, Joni can pray like a house on fire, and second, God is sovereign over people who don't even acknowledge Him. Did you know the word "sovereign" actually means "in control of everything"? Somebody needed to read that.

So God brought my kids back to me and we were suddenly sort of a crazy iteration of the Brady Bunch, minus Cindy. My ex and the kids moved into my old condo, and both Joni's children and mine attended the same school (which was another one of those "Joni" prayers I thought was just ridiculous at the time). Then my wife determined that she and my ex would begin meeting each week to read the Gospel of John together over lunch. You divorced guys let that last statement sink in for a minute. I was petrified. But as long as they didn't talk about me, I loved the idea. Amazingly, Joni even led my ex-wife in the prayer of salvation.

All was right with the world until November 28, 2007, when my ex-wife was diagnosed with Stage IV colon cancer, which had metastasized to her liver, lymph nodes, lungs, and kidneys. She was 42 years old. That night, she and I broke the news to our two children.

Within hours of leaving her apartment, I received a call from my son, Jordan. "Dad," he said, "Mom's moving back to Seattle, and I'm going with her." I was devastated. While my daughter would ultimately decide to move in with Joni and me, my son was leaving me again! I would be a liar if I said I wasn't mad at God. How could He miraculously bring my son back to me and then take him away again? What did I do?

I hurled my phone across the living room. Nolan Ryan couldn't have thrown a better fastball. With a crunch, my cell phone became plastic shrapnel as it slammed into our marble table. In a fury, I stormed out of the house, determined to stop that woman from taking my son out of the state of Florida yet again. Have you ever decided you had to drive somewhere to get your mind off your problems and found, no matter where you ended up, the problem just followed you? After aimlessly driving for what seemed like hours, I found myself calling my best friend, David.

"I need to come over," I blurted out.

"What's up?" was his confused reply.

Near tears, I simply reiterated, "I just need to come over."

Before I pulled into the driveway, I had already formulated a plan that involved David backing me up. I was going to enforce my divorce decree, which precluded my children from leaving the county, and I needed David's buy-in to make it fly. I knew I could count on him. But once we were inside his house, I just broke down. And you know what? David said nothing. He just got me some water and some tissues and listened to me ramble incoherently about how Jordan was leaving.

This is an excellent time for a reminder to Christian men everywhere. I can think of no other way to say it than "Bible bullets can be deadly." When faced with a crisis, a broken man doesn't need to hear your latest Scripture memorization or your theory on why things are falling apart. Broken men just need you to be there for them, period. Do you remember Job? That poor guy lost everything, from his children, to his home, to his business, to his investment portfolio (aka, "sheep"), to even his physical health. And Job had three friends who showed up in the midst of his pain and each had a differing opinion about why the man was suffering. One guy suggested it was Job's hidden sin, while another man thought perhaps it was the sin of his children that was the catalyst behind his trials. One man even had the audacity to proclaim that Job didn't understand God at all and to just deal with it.

However, in Job 2, the Bible makes it very clear that, before these three "church guys" stuck their collective feet in their mouths, they did something from which today's man could learn a lot. When these guys heard of Job's plight, they purposed themselves to go see him. They traveled a very long distance which, back in the days of camels and sandals, likely took a really long time. The Bible goes on to say:

> *When they saw him from a distance, they could hardly recognize him; they began to weep aloud, and they tore their robes and sprinkled dust on their heads. Then they sat on the ground with him for seven days and seven nights. No one said a word to him, because they saw how great his suffering was.*
>
> *Job 2:12-13*

They sat down with Job for a week and didn't say anything! One uninterrupted week of just feeling Job's pain without imparting any wisdom. Although they blew it later, they started out great! My friend did the same thing for me. Sometimes we just need someone to share airspace with us as we attempt to reconcile the trauma in our minds and hearts.

It wasn't until several hours had passed that David finally opened his mouth. "I was wondering why I was in Galatians this morning, and now I know why," he said. Did you know that sometimes, when we are immersed in the Word, it isn't intended for us? It may be for someone who we are going to encounter who needs to hear it, preferably at the appropriate time. After revealing that Galatians 3 spoke of Abraham, David asked, "What was Abraham's greatest test?" Well, I knew right away he was alluding to Abraham's calling to go to the Promised Land without so much as a suitcase. Boy, was I wrong. What David meant was the test of putting his own son, Issac, on an altar to be sacrificed to God.

My friend looked me square in the eye and said, "You have to let Jordan go. If you don't, and his mother dies, he will never forgive you." Well, so much for David accompanying me to the courthouse to file an injunction against my ex-wife. Indignantly, I argued that she was not allowed to leave with my son, but David wasn't buying it. After a prizefighter staredown, I conceded. And David was right.

Eighteen months to the day after her diagnosis, my ex-wife died. And God gave me my son back yet again. Only this time, it was for good. And we ended up with a very angry young man living under our roof. He hated me and hated Florida and didn't really want to be with us. He just punched holes in our walls and occasionally broke a finger on the stucco after losing his bout with our home's exterior. And the disappointment train rolled on.

No matter how hard I tried, we couldn't get Jordan to engage with the family or go to church with us. At that time in our lives, Joni and I were both serving on our church worship team, so we would take two vehicles to church. After the service, Joni would pile the other four kids in her car and I would go home and pick up Jordan for lunch. One Sunday in particular, I arrived at home to find my son decked out in a shirt that read "Marilize Liguana" surrounding a big green pot leaf. It doesn't take a decoder ring to figure out what that shirt said, and I was adamant when I said, "You are not wearing that shirt to lunch."

"Why, are you worried about what people will think of you? I hate it here! I hate you and I hate Joni!" he fired back.

As I stood at the bottom of the stairs, my son kicked a metal hamper into the drywall and defiantly flopped to the ground. All I could see were his knees sticking up as I heard him say, "Just go without me." So I left.

Fast forward ten minutes or so. I was parked under a tree and had sent Joni a text message that I would not be at lunch, nor would Jordan. Within seconds, she texted back words that stopped me in my tracks. "Why did Jordan just text his sister the word 'goodbye'?" it read. Breaking text protocol, I called her immediately, knowing my son was suicidal. You see, his heroes were all dead rock stars, and his favorite one was Kurt Cobain, the lead singer of the band Nirvana who, in 1994, had taken his own life with a shotgun blast to the head.

"I think Jordan is going to kill himself," I screamed into the phone. "I can't handle this one, Joni. Call the police and get home. If I walk in and find him dead on the floor, I will die right there with him. Please call me when you are inside so I know he's okay." So Joni took one for the team and called the sheriff's office. I vividly recalled Jordan telling his mom that if she went, he was going with her. Within minutes, she called me back. "They are going in now," she informed me. Looking back now, Joni had missed the part about calling AFTER they were inside, so now I was left knowing that when they entered my home, I would either hear my son's voice or my wife's scream.

And I heard his voice. "Son, were you trying to hurt yourself?" asked the deputy.

"Yes," Jordan answered.

"Have you thought about this before?" the sheriff asked.

"Yes," replied my son.

"Would you like some help, son?" was the final question.

Over the phone, Joni informed me they were going to exercise the Baker Act and take Jordan away for 72 hours. "Don't let them leave before I see him," I yelled.

I swear I came into my neighborhood on two wheels. I dodged the first police car, which blocked my road, and slid up behind the second cruiser, which blocked my driveway and which also had my son in the back seat in handcuffs. I ran to the car, grabbed his neck, and said, "You're my only son; you're my only son." And for a brief moment, I think I knew how God felt as Jesus went to the cross, only my son didn't have to die on that day.

"Call David! Call David," Joni barked as I lost my mind in the living room. I was catatonic and thought I was going to have a heart attack. My wife knows that when the odds are insurmountable, I need to call David. Joni knows when she's the wrong person for the job, and she is confident David and I can survive anything as long as we are back to back. You know, I would imagine that the only way my friend even knew it was me was by the caller ID on his phone, since all I did was sob into his earpiece. He didn't ask me anything but rather started to pray. And pray and pray. Not until I received a call waiting beep from the suicide center did I ultimately break my silence.

Ever so calmly, the lady on the phone informed me that we were to bring Jordan three changes of clothing and some food. Joni and I bolted out of the house, picked up some McDonald's, and headed to the center. Sitting across from me, on a hard plastic chair and wearing no shoelaces, was my little boy. He was sobbing and begging me to take him home. Any dad who hears "I don't wanna be here, Daddy" usually wants to pull an "Arnold Schwarzenegger" and blast an escape hole in the wall, but I knew I had to leave Jordan there.

I was asked a battery of questions, including: "Has there been any recent major change in his life?" (He had just moved across the country for the fourth time in a decade), "Has he experienced any significant loss lately?" (His mother just died, for crying out loud), and "How is his relationship with his stepmother?" (It really couldn't have been much worse). All in all, he was a textbook suicide candidate. After kissing him goodbye, Joni and I left for what would be the longest night of my life.

Surprisingly, I received a call the very next afternoon. The doctor on the phone informed me that Jordan was free to leave and further stated he was not suicidal but just sad and incapable of dealing with the loss of his mother. So I called David to update him and ask for prayer, and then I struck out to get my boy. He met me at the door, smiling, and he simply asked if he could see Joni. You can imagine my surprise and the sudden fear that overtook me as I determined he no longer wanted to kill himself, but her instead. "Why do you want to do that?" I asked.

Almost begging, Jordan again asked to go see his stepmother. I obliged, and when he saw her, he ran over to her and hugged her. It was a long hug, and I heard him say, "I'm sorry." I just sort of looked at my kid like a puppy looks at you when it hears a funny noise, head cocked to one side with that "what the...?" look on its face. I was dumbfounded, to say the least. What happened to my son?

Afterward, I looked at my son like he had three heads. "What was that all about?" I asked. Jordan proceeded to tell me that, when he was taken back to the "unit" to join seven other troubled kids, he was informed by one of his compatriots that if he wasn't honest with the doctors, he would be stuck there "forever." I don't know if what this guy told my son was accurate, but it put the fear of God into Jordan. And it's a good thing, because I had completed a 24-page questionnaire during our initial visit, so the battery of physicians had some pretty precise info.

Then Jordan shared that one of his "cellmates" was homicidal, one had parents who had been providing him with drugs, one had a mother who had tried to kill him, while yet another had completed his 72 hours and his folks refused to pick him up. Along with the roomful of questionable people, my son also told me they were told what to watch on TV and when to go to sleep. At bedtime, Jordan was placed in solitary, with no light. In fact, he alluded to the fact he couldn't see his hand in front of his face.

Summing up his 24 hours of incarceration, Jordan simply said, "After hearing what these other kids were going through, I realized I didn't have it bad. You and Joni love me; I have a bed and my computer. Yeah, Mom's dead, but my life isn't that bad."

Immediately after his release, he began to integrate with our family a little more. He became active in the youth ministry at our church and even started a ministry designed to reach out to young people whose parents are suffering or were lost as a result of terminal cancer. I truly believe God grabbed my son in the middle of a dark room, all alone. Much like me, God Himself reached out to Jordan. No evangelist, no church… just sheer desperation.

Two very big light bulbs came on for me after withstanding the drama of losing my son geographically and of almost losing him physically. First, I would have never made it without David. God put us together, back to back, for battle, and Lord knows we have both had our fair share.

Secondly, God revealed something to me about the trials we go through as men, whether a teenager or an adult. It is more than likely you have been through some pretty awful stuff, as both my son and I have. God gives us a choice when we finally emerge from the winter season and spring comes. We can either give it away or die with it.

God wants us to use our survival skills to aid other men. Let me put some wheels underneath this concept. If you wanted to climb Mt. Everest, you wouldn't jump off the plane and head up the trail toward the summit. More than likely, you would hire a local Nepalese guide, who had climbed that mountain a hundred times, to lead you to the precipice. That guide knows which steps will lead you safely upward and which will result in you plummeting thousands of feet. Why? Because he's been there.

You have been given the gift of going through some hard-fought battles. Don't waste it. Grab a rope, lash it to a man who's going through the exact same thing God brought you through, and lead him to safety. Men need other men for support when a situation seems more than hopeless. We desperately need someone to drag us out of the jungle after we have had our legs blown off by the landmines of life. And with the other guy, and the Lord, we can and we will survive. Remember that:

> *Though one may be overpowered, two can defend themselves. A cord of three strands is not quickly broken.*
>
> *Ecclesiastes 4:12*

Activation Questions

- *Have I ever suffered through a crisis alone? How did I deal with it?*

- *Do I think I may have come away better if I had walked through it with another man?*

- *What key past crisis in my life would be valuable to another man, if I could share it with others with no fear of judgment?*

5.

WINGMAN? WHAT WINGMAN?
(The Dreaded Accountability Discussion)

While support and cover fire are critical to survival, so is personal discipline and accountability. Any man who has been through boot camp will tell you that the drill sergeant is one tough dude. Ironically, after polling a lot of men, I often discover most high school athletic coaches find their way onto their "Top 10 People Who Influenced My Life" lists. I remember hating my track coach in high school, mumbling about his mother as I ran yet another two miler. After all, I was a sprinter (with some pretty bad shin splints, I might add), so what the heck was I running two miles for? But that man taught me how to endure pain and persist through exhaustion, and he even corrected my block start so I got a better launch when the pistol fired.

An integral part of any relationship with another Kingdom guy involves extending permission for him to call us into account when appropriate. In other words, you give this guy the green light to tell you when you're being a complete moron. And perhaps the most important rule regarding this component of being connected to another guy is just doing what he suggests, whether you agree with it or not. Remember when David told me I had to let my son leave? It went against everything I wanted, but I listened to him and it worked out pretty well, disregarding the whole suicidal season in the middle of it all.

I can think of no better illustration of the importance of listening to the other guy than Pete "Maverick" Mitchell from the movie *Top Gun*. Now Maverick wasn't exactly humble, having been accused of having an ego that was "writing checks his body can't cash." He was the son of an F-4 Phantom pilot who had been shot down in combat, and Maverick's mission appeared to be to fly better than his dad. But because he was egomaniacal and had a very pronounced tendency to "go it alone," Mitchell got himself into more than a few scrapes with his commanding officers and even his own Radar Intercept Officer (RIO), "Goose."

Through a series of very fortunate events, Maverick and Goose find themselves at Fighter Weapons School, or "Top Gun," in Miramar, California. Top Gun consists of the top 1% of all naval aviators who spend weeks honing their skills in air-to-air combat, or "dogfighting." There they meet Iceman, a notorious pilot who is the presumed winner of the coveted Top Gun trophy before the competition even starts. Maverick, along with the massive chip on his shoulder, refuses to acknowledge many of the rules put in place for safety and has a bad habit of showboating.

Since aerial dogfighting has become a lost art, Top Gun pilots are drilled continuously using different aircraft combinations. In one scene, Maverick and Goose are paired up with Hollywood and Wolfman in two F-14 Tomcats, facing "Jester" (the Top Gun Executive Officer) and "Viper" (the CO of Top Gun). There are some cardinal rules in dogfighting, one of which is you stick together as a team to prevent losing your combined aircraft.

At the outset of this particular scene, Maverick and Hollywood are engaged with Jester. Hollywood is on Jester's tail, and Maverick is covering Hollywood's wing. Upon seeing Viper off on the horizon, Maverick opts to break off and pursue Viper. Before banking away, Goose, who happens to be riding shotgun with Maverick, cautions his pilot, "Don't leave Hollywood, Mav. We're covering his wing." Then Hollywood chimes in from next door, "Don't you leave me, Maverick." After surveying the situation and doing a quick once-over of Hollywood's aircraft, Maverick says, "Hollywood. You're looking good. I'm going after Viper." Abandoning his responsibility to his wingman, he rockets into pursuit of his commanding officer.

Let me pause here to ask a question: Have you ever shaken the hand of the usher or the greeter at church on a Sunday morning? You look at him with your best game face on, and he looks back at you with his as he says, "Welcome to church," and hands you the day's bulletin. He looks good, all dressed in his usher's uniform (aka, a suit) and you are in your Sunday best also. And the dialogue ends. After all, he looks good, just like Hollywood. Maverick glanced in the direction of Hollywood before heading off after Viper, and he made the assumption the pilot was just fine. I mean, his plane had wings and it was still airborne, so Hollywood should have been great. How can we possibly ascertain how this usher in a suit is doing simply by looking at his clothing? Next time, ask him how he's really doing. It may take time out of your race to the pew, but you may just discover how "not fine" he really is. He needs a wingman, too.

Back to our story. Impressed by his flying skills, Viper continues the run away from Maverick. And consumed with nothing more than a vision to shoot down the boss man, Maverick chases him relentlessly. Every so often, you hear Viper egging his protégé on, "C'mon, Mav. Keep comin,'" he says to himself.

With no advanced notice whatsoever, Maverick's missile warning system engages and is locked onto by Jester, who dutifully pulls the simulated trigger. In the real world, Maverick and Goose are officially dead. And so are Hollywood and Wolfman.

You know, I am not sure the creator of *Top Gun* had any idea of the biblical connotation of the name "Viper." Viper, serpent, snake... Satan. And, in many ways, the "Viper" in *Top Gun* operates just like the enemy of our souls. Think about it. The pilot Viper knew how Maverick would react before the wheels on their respective planes were even off of the runway. Viper knew Maverick's ego and also knew Maverick, if properly motivated, would leave his wingman duties to chase after him. And at the end of the scene, both Maverick and his wingman are dead, at least on paper.

Satan works exactly the same way when it comes to men. He studies us and always seems to know the best "bait" to use on us. He's the ultimate fisherman, knowing which bait will cause us to open our mouth and get hooked. Satan will work a plan of putting something in front of us that will inspire us to abandon our post, so to speak. I believe one of Satan's key missions is to isolate men from other men. When we are alone, we are more prone to sin. So, like Viper, Satan slowly leads us away from other guys. "That's good, man. Keep comin,'" he'll say, until we are miles away from anyone. And an isolated man, just like Hollywood or Maverick, is an easy target. Do you realize that, when a wolf wants to kill a sheep, it very methodically separates it from the flock? Satan's role is that of a wolf—to get us alone and spiritually kill us. The key to survival is to stay tight with our wingman.

What's even worse about Maverick's decision is that he was warned multiple times to stay put. First, Goose yells at him from the same cockpit. Then Hollywood, the hapless wingman, begs Maverick to not leave him alone. But all Maverick can see is the "bigger, better deal." He is determined to shoot down Viper, even if it kills him.

A word of caution. If you have an accountability partner and he implores you NOT to do something, listen to the man. His role in your life is to keep you from making an unrecoverable mistake. When we enter into the covenant of friendship, or in this case a "wingman," we commit to listening to what the guy tells us. There is wisdom in a multitude of counsel, and our success is our wingman's goal.

Have you ever heard of a guy named Eldrick Tont Woods? Let me give you a hint. He has won more than a dozen major golf championships, 16 World Golf Championships, and he has been the PGA Player of the Year a record 10 times. If you have yet to figure it out, it's Tiger Woods. This guy has some impressive golf statistics, including winning the Byron Nelson Award for lowest adjusted scoring average eight times and leading the money list in nine different seasons. In the world of golf, this guy is legend.

Tiger does, however, carry with him one number that I am sure he would prefer be long forgotten. The number is 11. On December 11, 2009, Woods announced he would take an indefinite leave from the game of golf to work on his marriage after admitting infidelity. If memory serves, he "admitted" infidelity after being chased down the driveway by his wife, Elin, who ultimately beat his face in with a 4-iron through the window of his

Cadillac Escalade. The number of women who came forward, implicating Tiger? Eleven.

There is a saying I live by every day: "Those who have nothing to hide, hide nothing." Tiger didn't get caught with his pants down in some seedy hotel or out at a bar in some far-off city, but rather via an errant text message from one of his "other women." He inadvertently left his cell phone on the table, and his wife read it, which resulted in her stellar swing into her husband's mug. A word to the wise: If your wife can't see all of your messages, then make some changes. I do believe Tiger Woods would tell you the same thing since he lost his wife, his kids, and a large percentage of his income.

Here's what really blows my mind. Tiger Woods had women all over the country, some working at diners, while others worked at exotic dance places and even in adult film. And he also had a posse of people, from paparazzi to desperate golf club salesmen, that tailed him everywhere. I mean, the guy had a caddy who followed him all over the golf course and offered counsel on which way the green was breaking and which club to use. Do you mean to tell me that, with all of those fans and staff, no one saw anything or, worse yet, said anything?

Think about this for a minute. What if—and I mean it's a big "what if," considering many of the people in question were on his payroll—someone had approached Tiger and said, "Mr. Woods, I know there may be nothing going on when you sneak out the back door of the restaurant with that waitress, but it doesn't look good"? Notice that there's no conviction or condemnation in those words, but rather an alert that people are watching (and perhaps drawing their own conclusions). The person didn't need to say, "Hey, dude, knock it off," because the evidence was clearly circumstantial. But to call attention to the questionable behavior may have been just enough to avert certain disaster. This is what an accountability partner is for. Not to judge or to rebuke, but to put a spotlight on words or behaviors that may contradict what God says and may ultimately put us in some sort of jeopardy.

There is a similar recount in the Bible in 2 Samuel 11. Actually, the first verse is really the kiss of death for King David:

> *In the spring, at the time when kings go off to war, David sent Joab out with the king's men and the whole Israelite army. They destroyed the Ammonites and besieged Rabbah. But David remained in Jerusalem.*
>
> *2 Samuel 11:1*

Notice the verse says that in the spring, kings went off to war. And the last sentence simply states that David hung out in Jerusalem while his general, Joab, went out and got the job done against the enemy. So if all kings go off to war, and David was indeed the king of Israel, then why did he decide to call in sick? What was he thinking? This, unfortunately, led to a series of massive missteps by the "man after God's own heart."

If you have ever read of King David, you may remember he makes a series of blunders which increase in magnitude. First, while sitting at home, the king decides to walk out onto his balcony only to spot a woman in a bathtub (outside?). Then he inquires about her and ultimately has a servant bring the woman to him. He commits adultery with the woman named Bathsheba and desires to be with her for good. Unfortunately, Bathsheba is already married to Uriah the Hittite, who is out on the front lines fighting for Israel at this time.

Sinking deeper still, David implores Uriah to return from the battlefield for a day's rest, hoping that the soldier will hang out with Bathsheba long enough to get her pregnant and thereby cover the king's tracks. But instead of going home, Uriah decides to spend the night outside of the city gate to protect David from harm. And, as thanks for his dedication to David, Uriah is sent out to the front lines of battle and ultimately dies after his entire unit strands him. And David gets the girl.

We really don't know much about Uriah, and we have but brief snapshots of King David's life. But, rest assured, David and Uriah were more than just acquaintances. You see, Uriah was actually one of King David's Mighty Men. There were only 30 of these Mighty Men and, suffice it to say, they were the king's elite fighting machines, aiding David in strategizing and executing battle plans. King David and Uriah the Hittite were buddies. For all we know, David may have even been at Uriah and Bathsheba's wedding.

Sin got the best of one of God's most adept warriors, which means none of us are immune from being attacked by the enemy or suffering from temporary spiritual insanity. David made a series of decisions that went from bad to worse, and there were some steep consequences from the Lord, not to mention he lost a close friend.

Granted the relationship between David and Bathsheba, however inappropriate it was, somehow led to the lineage of Jesus Christ, but consider this. Much like Tiger Woods, what if someone had noticed the king up on the balcony that day? What if that person knocked on the David's door and simply said, "With all due respect, King, why aren't you at work today?" Perhaps the entire relational disaster could have been averted.

No man is designed to travel alone or battle without covering fire. And no man is truly safe without authentic friendship. Without someone watching our back and, when necessary, questioning our motives or actions, it's not a matter of "if" we will fall but "when." We don't just need men to cover our backs but to also make sure that we don't shoot ourselves in the foot with our own mistakes.

Accountability is a non-negotiable battle asset.

Activation Questions

- *Have I ever felt as if a man I met was hurting? What did I do? Would I do it differently now?*

- *Looking back at my life, what's the biggest mistake I have made that I likely would not have made had someone said "Don't do it!"?*

- *Is there a man in my life I trust to give me good counsel when I feel off track?*

6.

YOU DON'T QUIT ON ME!
(Every Man's Need for Encouragement)

It has happened to me at least once every year for the past seven years. After all, I have five teenagers, two college tuitions, a mortgage, bills.... and I'm in full-time domestic missions. "I quit," I murmur dejectedly. "I just want a 9-to-5 job and a paycheck, and I just want to do the Sunday church gig like all of my friends." Some of you overly pious types will ask me where my trust in the Lord is, but I would be willing to bet you've been there, too, especially in today's economy.

This year was no different. Everything was falling apart around me. I was suffocating under the vast array of spiritual leader responsibilities and I was done. To make matters worse, I had a meeting that night with my board of directors. Honestly, the last thing I wanted that night were people in my house when I was completely defeated. I really didn't feel like going on and had this overwhelming desire to watch '80s movies and just check out. I'll get back to that in a minute...

On a different track, I'm sure you'll agree there is one thing missing from the world of Hollywood filmmakers and that is simply good, God-honoring motion pictures with biblical values. Most of the junk on the big screen is exactly that: junk. There is, however, one emerging exception to this stigma. That would be the guys at Sherwood Baptist Church in Albany, Georgia, who have created great movies like *Courageous, Fireproof,* and *Facing the Giants.*

Taking on the proverbial Goliath, little Sherwood Pictures put together *Facing the Giants* with a budget of only $100,000. But the football flick went on to break down the barriers of its predecessors to earn more than $10 million at the box office. Since the cast was comprised almost exclusively of Albany locals and Sherwood congregants, the filmmakers were forced to shoot only a section of bleachers at a time. There weren't enough people to fill the stands, so they would ask the extras to move from grandstand to grandstand as the ball moved down the field to give the illusion of a packed house. While that has nothing to do with my point, I just love how creative the Kendrick brothers were as they made this revolutionary film about defeat and victory.

If you've seen the movie, you're likely no stranger to the "death crawl" scene. The clip is frequently used to illustrate leadership. *Rough Cut Men* uses it a little differently, with the dialogue during the scene being the focal point.

Brock Kelley is a hard-nosed linebacker who has already all but checked out of the season after the Shiloh Christian Academy has suffered major off-season losses to their roster. The kid does everything possible to be a dark cloud over the team, and Coach Grant Taylor, while seeing Brock's potential, has had enough of his mouth. After a grueling team "death crawl," where larger players carry lighter players on their backs down the football field, Coach Taylor gets caught up in yet another defeatist discussion with Brock.

Finally arriving at wit's end with his linebacker, the coach invites Brock onto the field for yet another death crawl, with a wide receiver named Jeremy on his back.

Brock: I can make it to the 30.

Coach Taylor: I think you can make it to the 50.

Brock: I can make it to the 50 with nobody on my back.

Taylor: I think you can make it to the 50 with Jeremy on your back. But no matter what happens, I want you to give me your best.

Brock: Okay.

Taylor: You're going to give me your best?

Brock: *[growing tired of the question]* I'm gonna give you my best.

Taylor: Okay. But just to make sure, I want you do it blindfolded.

Brock: Why?

Taylor: Because I don't want you giving up on me at a certain point...

If you notice the above dialogue, there is nothing more than simple conviction and a challenge put forth by Coach Taylor. He doesn't call Brock "lazy" or a "loser" but simply throws down the gauntlet, and Brock accepts. Every guy loves a good challenge, regardless of how hard we think it might be. It's in our DNA.

So, blindfolded, Brock strikes off down the football field with Jeremy hanging on for dear life to Brock's shoulder pads. Ten yards, 20 yards, 30 yards—his teammates are on the sideline heckling him. Forty yards, 50 yards, 60 yards—his fellow players are standing up, watching in growing awe. All the while, Brock's arms are burning and he can't see where he's going. At 70 yards, Brock's tune changes from one of cocky self-assuredness to downright defeat. Then comes the pain at 80 yards and the near failure of his arms at 90 yards. Coach Taylor prods Brock for another 10 steps, and the exhausted linebacker goes face-down in the turf.

"Look up, Brock. You're in the end zone."

This kid had predetermined he might get 30 yards as a pair of players and half the field with no human backpack, but he made it the entire length of the field. Was it his superhuman arm strength? Probably not. Was it the crowd yelling at him as he churned down the field? Maybe, but only as a partial contributor. Was it Wheaties? Nope.

It was that coach. Granted, this is a textbook superior/subordinate relationship. We all know that the coach is supposed to push his players hard. But it's the progression of the dialogue that is so crucial and worth emulating as we work with that guy God puts in our lives when he's ready to throw in the towel.

Let me give you the yardage replay and include the words of Coach Taylor this time as Brock is moving down the field. Ten yards, 20 yards, 30 yards—"Don't stop. You gotta keep moving, Brock. Let's go, let's go, let's go!" Forty yards, 50 yards, 60 yards—"That's it, Brock! Keep moving! A little bit more. You're looking good!" By 70 yards, Brock is hurting a little. "I'm not quitting. I'm just resting a little." Coach Taylor just keeps him moving in spite of the imminent cramping. By 80 yards, Brock is ready to give up: "It hurts. My arms hurt." And by 90 yards, Coach Taylor is also down on his knees, urging into his player's ear, "Then you negotiate with your body to find more strength, but you don't give up on me."

Over the last 10 grueling yards of this impromptu 100-yard death crawl, Brock is near sobbing and begging to be done, while Coach Taylor is saying (more like screaming), "Don't quit! Don't quit! Don't quit! Five more steps! Four more steps! Don't quit!"

Even in the arena of peer-to-peer relationships, men need an encourager. We need that guy who won't let us give up, quit, or bail. This man knows the true meaning of perseverance and the results of it:

> *Not only so, but we also rejoice in our sufferings, because we know that suffering produces perseverance; perseverance, character; and character, hope.*

> *Romans 5:3-4*

This man is our Barnabas, our encourager. He has our best interests in mind and won't take "I give up" or "I quit" as an option. There's no turning in our man card when this man is on watch.

So in spite of my whining during our board meeting, and since David (my accountability partner) is also the vice president of our ministry and chairman of our board of directors, you can probably assume I wasn't going to get out of my duties or my calling that easily. After the meeting ended and we were alone, my wife remained seated to my right, with David sitting to my left. There's nothing like getting caught between your wife and your accountability partner. Talk about a "no wimp zone."

"You have had a cloud over you this entire meeting," David said, "You didn't even seem like you wanted to be here and it's your ministry."

Joni, on my opposite side, just said "Yeah!"

"Great," I thought to myself. "I've been had."

One thing worthy of mention when it comes to your wing-man is that it is a safe place to just be you. No mask, no BS, just straight shooting. I told David I was exhausted. I was try-ing to balance a family, and a very heavy travel schedule, cou-pled with some major "kid issues" and not enough money to pay the bills... again. I started to cry mid-sentence, and instead of a barrage of "coulda, shoulda, woulda," I was the recipient of compassion and empathy.

At that moment, both my bride and my buddy reminded me we had never missed a meal, God always provides, and a litany of the usual Christian pep talk. But, for some odd reason, when it came from David and my wife, I actually got it. I wiped my tears, Joni hugged me, and I felt a little better. But honestly, I was still exhausted and really saw no solution to the latest problems.

Without much else, David jumped up and informed us he had to get home. As he was packing up to leave, he turned around and said, "Question for you..." I knew I was in trou-ble, because whenever he said that, I knew he knew I already knew the answer. He just wanted to hear me say it, whatever it was.

"How's your time in the Word been lately?" he asked. I dug deep for my best excuse, since it had been at least a month since I had cracked open my Bible.

"I've been so busy that I haven't had time," I replied.

"And are you tithing?" he fired.

Ugh. Now I was really in for it. "We never have enough money for the bills, much less tithing," I answered confidently. Now that was weak... I could stand in front of hundreds of men and tell them to tithe, but I wasn't practicing what I was preach-ing, literally, and David knew it.

"Well, that's the problem. My work is done here," David said as he walked out the door.

Beginning the following day, I got back into the disciplines of reading and tithing. Currently, I have even gotten to a point of tithing the first tenth of my week, eight hours, every Monday, to God. Sure, I slip up once in a while, but David is right there to question me about it and I just hate telling that guy when I've let it slide.

And this book? For months, David was all over me about writing it. So was my wife. They both wanted it written, and making excuses was not a viable option for me. David enlightened me to the fact that writing, like working out at the gym, is a discipline. You do it even when you don't feel like it. He once asked me, "Do you think you can write three pages a day? It doesn't have to be perfect, just write something?" I agreed, and commencing the next day, and the day after that, I received a perfectly timed text message that simply read "three pages." That dude reminded me every single day about those stupid three pages for months. And God help me if the answer was "not today."

Whenever I am ready to give up yet again, David is right there to get me through. Sure, he beats on me when I screw up, and he supports me back to back. But he also plays an invaluable role in my life when I can't move another inch. Through his words and actions, he often reminds me:

We are hard pressed on every side, but not crushed; perplexed, but not in despair; persecuted, but not abandoned; struck down, but not destroyed.

2 Corinthians 4:8-9

As paradoxical as it sounds, David is actually my Jonathan. He loves me as himself, and when I hurt, he hurts. And vice versa. Your "Jonathan" will probably always point you right back to God. He will remind you of how far you've come, will carry you when you are feeling defeated, and will fire you up when you are unmotivated.

God has an encourager, a coach, a supporter, and a hall monitor for you. It's just a matter of finding him and beginning a relationship that can transform your walk with Jesus and make you a better man, a better husband, and a better father.

The trick is figuring out how to find him.

Activation Questions

- *Have I ever quit something mid-stream? How did it go down?*

- *Am I facing a battle today that I am ready to just give up on? It could be a job, kids or even your marriage…*

- *Have I ever told another man about it? If not, why not?*

7.

BOOK 'EM, DANNO!
(Developing an Authentic Friendship)

Probably the most frequent question I get asked, either during or after a *Rough Cut Men* event is "How do you even begin to find a guy to go to war with?" I hear it more so after telling them the tales of how David has pulled me through some really tough times. By the way, our friendship is reciprocal, but since I'm really only a subject expert on me, I am focusing my energy on my trials as opposed to his. I may run past a few of his struggles on the fly just to illustrate how our relationship has morphed over the years, but most of what you will read is pretty one-sided.

All that aside, here's the bottom line. At some point after we graduate from high school or college and enter the marketplace in whatever capacity we choose, we become almost completely incapable of making friends. I think this is partly due to time constraints, while fear and embarrassment and even a little stranger anxiety can work into the mix. We have become a nation of "strong, silent types," which is actually contrary to how God designed us as men. Somehow, we need to get back to the concept of "playground" friendships.

When I was in kindergarten, we played a really cool game on the playground. It was *Hawaii 5-0*. Now there has been a second iteration of this Hawaiian-based police drama, but it's just not the same thing. This was the original late '60s, early '70s show. In hindsight, I don't think any of my six-year-old friends were actually allowed to watch that show, especially since it was way past our collective bedtimes. But we still had police chases, complete with authentic siren sounds, and spoke on car phones with ivy branches for cords (which were connected to absolutely nothing, just like McGarrett's handset).

We let anyone play that game, and the only time we ever experienced any real drama was when it came to selecting who would be McGarrett and who would be Danno. If you remember the show, you may also remember that McGarrett's tagline was "Book'em, Danno." No one ever actually wanted to be Danno, because he always had to do the grunt work and never got to speak those famous words. But, you know, we didn't discriminate. Anyone could join the game. All that they had to do was walk up and ask, "Can I play?" because there was always room for more "townspeople" and "henchmen" on our roster.

Developing an accountable relationship with a guy is just like playing *Hawaii 5-0* The problem with us church guys is we try to over-spiritualize everything, or we just make it too difficult. This isn't about a curriculum, programming, or holding hands in prayer, but rather just being friends. Remember friends?

I went to work for David in 2004, as a new home salesman. He was the builder and I was one of his associates, which made it about as superior/subordinate as you can get. I answered to him for my performance and for the progress of construction, and when I first interviewed with him, I knew this guy was a believer. If you were thinking it was because of his demeanor or some peaceful thing about his spirit, you'd be wrong. He actually had this big cross on his computer screen, so I put two and two together.

In my opinion, my boss was a spiritual giant. I mean, David was actually in the process of memorizing the entire Gospel of John. Yeah, that's right, all 21 chapters. He prayed constantly, was always on his A-game as a husband, and never even said a bad word. It was comical in' some ways, because I idolized the guy and thought to myself, "If I could be half the Christian David is, I'd be awesome!"

As men, I think we occasionally set ourselves up for disappointment when we try to be more like another Christian instead of more Christ-like, and I learned this firsthand when I heard that my boss, in a fit of anger, had punched a hole in a door. While I was concerned about his damaged digits, inside I said, "YES! He's normal!" That was the day the ground at the foot of the cross became level between me and my boss, David.

While it was encouraging to work for a Christian builder, the accountability part of our relationship emerged somewhat accidentally. It was during the heyday of new home sales in Florida, a time where selling a home every day was not uncommon. I was on the phone with my wife, having a heated discussion about something totally irrelevant and unmemorable, and my volume had sharply increased during the call. I looked up to see David standing at the door of my office, shuffling through papers.

"Put the phone on hold," he motioned.

"Yes!" I thought to myself as I put Joni on hold. "He's going to tell me about another contract I just closed!"

As dollar signs flooded my mind, David asked, "Who are you talking to like that on the phone?"

"It's Joni," I replied.

"If you ever talk to your wife like that again in my office, you're fired," he said. And thus began my accountable Christian relationship with David.

Where it went from there is a literal whirlwind of change. In only a few short years, I was called into ministry. I recall a breakfast meeting with David, where I informed him that I was being called into full-time ministry. His only question to me was why I hadn't left already, as he was fully aware of the call. You see, I owed David thousands of dollars on "draws versus commission" (I had been paid for homes that hadn't closed at the bank yet), and I felt obligated to stick it out in spite of my marching orders from God.

"David," he said, "I am only a steward of God's money. That debt is forgiven and you don't owe me a thing. Now what's stopping you?" This was the moment when we crossed over from boss vs. employee to David and Jonathan.

Our friendship has covered a lot of ground, and it has been coupled with a lot of significant life changes. With the collapse of the real estate market, David and I spent countless hours together in prayer as he agonized over a decision to shut down his business, which he ultimately did. We have been through the cross-country exploits of my son several times and the suicide disaster that ensued. We have been through the deaths of both of our mothers-in-law, exactly one year apart, and have dealt with the grieving of our respective wives afterward.

In fact, there was an interesting component of our friendship that emerged as a result of the loss of both David's wife's mother and Joni's mother. His mother-in-law had succumbed to a long battle with cancer in 2007, while my mother-in-law died quite suddenly of sepsis in December of 2008. I recall being with Joni in the hospital room for hours as her mother got worse, then got better, then got worse, then became peaceful. I had left that intensive care unit with my mother-in-law improving, only to receive a text from my wife mere minutes later that simply read, "She's gone, honey." As I wandered the halls of the hospital, I called David to let him know what had happened. And he offered counsel I will never forget.

Believe it or not, David proceeded to coach me on what NOT to say to my wife. He made sure I knew not to tell her that her mom was in a better place, or that she wasn't in pain any more, or that now she had a new body. He was clear, crystal clear, that now was not the time to get all hyper-biblical but rather to just serve my wife. And you know what? I probably would have said EXACTLY what David told me not to say had he not cautioned me against it beforehand.

Developing an authentic relationship takes time. As trust develops, the depth of the discussions drive deeper and the element of accountability becomes a natural by-product. It isn't a relationship that can be forced, mandated, or suggested as a part of a program or a curriculum. Frankly, we men aren't like women. We won't just cry on another person's shoulders about all of our junk. However, we are more likely to lock shields in the battle with a guy that we trust.

Discipleship is a result of relationship, not the inverse. Shoving guys into small groups will result in awkward discussions, superficial topics, and high attrition rates as men stop showing up. It's really, in a way, similar to a marriage covenant. You each commit to confidentiality, depth, compassion, and absolutely no judgment.

Think about this. Most of our experiences in the church, especially when it comes to connecting with other men, rely almost exclusively on the once-per-month breakfast and the compulsory Bible study/prayer meeting. It's a recipe for disaster if you put this into a dating relationship of sorts. It would be like asking your best girl on a date, picking her up for a one-hour breakfast date, and dropping her off an hour later. But before you part ways, you commit to picking her at the same time on the first of the following month. Now exactly how much of a relationship can guys build when they see each other once a month? Especially when it occurs in a time-stringent format with little room for real discussion?

Here's the true equation: Time equals trust and trust builds relationship. And, as I mentioned a few paragraphs ago, relationship breeds discipleship. I know what you may be thinking. "How do I connect with a guy like this guy has?" On the surface, it may seem daunting, but it's really pretty simple. Just hang out together. Friendship develops through common interests and sharing the same air space. And just like dating, there are guys who are a good fit and a bad fit. That sort of shakes itself out. Trust me.

Contrary to most traditional men's ministry visions, do you know that David and I have never done a Bible study together? Sure, we've prayed together until we were both hoarse, but we've never agreed to read the same Christian men's book and then break it down every week. In fact, we don't even go to the same church or run with the same guys. No format and no program. We meet with a purpose, but we never have an agenda. I'm sure you'll agree there's a huge difference between the two.

We know when we are meeting, but that's typically just about it. We decide where to eat and let God lead us. Invariably, one of us is usually the "dumper" (the guy having a terrible week) and the other is the "dumpee" (the sounding board). In a nutshell, we listen, we counsel, and we call to account if the other guy is way off base. It's really that easy.

Understandably, the most difficult part in bridging from Bible study partners to boots-on-the-ground warriors is asking another guy to join you. Imagine the response you might get if you walked up a man in your Bible study and said, "Hey, Bob. You and I have been in a small group together for five years. I really need a friend and I think it's time to take our relationship to the *next level.*" If he's armed, he just might fire. Let's face it; we live in a homophobic culture where dudes hugging in a Denny's parking lot can really send up red flags (especially if you live in the Deep South like I do).

My suggestion, just based on personal experience, is to pray hard for God to bring the right guy into your life. Then just keep doing what you're doing. Your "Jonathan" may just materialize when you are at a football game or some other "non-church" event. After all, Christian men are in the world the other six days of the week, too. My guess is you already know someone whom God has put on your heart. Your job is to truthfully tell him of your latest challenge and solicit his input. We guys love it when someone asks for help since we're inherent "fixers." I would surmise you will find that he has as many battles as you, and the rocket launch of authentic friendship will begin its countdown.

More than likely, some of the really holy guys reading this are dying for me to back up my points with Scripture. This is a book for Christian guys, after all, and it sounds like a relationship handbook so far.

First and foremost, let me say our God is a God of relationships. The principal mission of God's son, Jesus Christ, was to build a bridge between a fallen man and a Holy God. And He dutifully sent His only Son to die on a cross so we could have an authentic and real relationship with our Creator. And God wants us connected to His kids, too.

At the very beginning of everything, in Genesis, God created everything, right? Each successive day, God began to unpack the world as we see it. Day one, He made light. Day two, it was sky and seas. Then land, plants, the sun and the moon, animals, and finally man. If you read Genesis 1, you will actually notice that, almost every day, God looked at His accomplishments and called them "good" or even "very good." At only one point in the process of creation did the Creator notice that something in His handiwork was "not good":

> *The Lord God said, "It is not good for the man to be alone.*
> *I will make a helper suitable for him.*
>
> *Genesis 2:18*

In this case, we know his "helper" refers to Eve, Adam's wife. But the overarching sentiment, pronounced by God Himself, indicates it was never His intention for man to be by himself. It dates back to the first guy who walked the planet, and it still applies to us today.

God's relational superstructure is contingent upon people being connected. We've done a fantastic job of meeting in churches by the hundreds, but the one-on-one component has been largely overlooked. When Jesus sent out His first disciples into a mission field that we are still charged with today, he had a very simple formula for success:

> *After this the Lord appointed seventy-two others and sent them two by two ahead of him to every town and place where he was about to go.*

Luke 10:1

Notice that Jesus doesn't send out teams of 20 or stadiums of 20,000 but rather two at a time. Jesus knew that men traveling alone were prone to attack, and perhaps even failure, without the necessary backup.

Following the lead laid down by His Savior, the apostle Paul executed his missions in a similar manner. Shortly after his sudden salvation, the self-professed "head Pharisee" met Barnabas. And the two of them struck out on mission together. At some point, there was a bit of a role reversal between the two men, with Paul assuming command. But at the end of the day, these two men stayed together.

As an encouragement to today's Christian man, it's nice to know that even Paul and Barnabas didn't have a utopian relationship. When John Mark (also known as "Mark"—you may have read his Gospel) joined the two missionaries and subsequently decided to bail out in the middle of the trip, it sparked controversy. So much so that when planning their second mission, Paul and Barnabas vehemently disagreed as to whether Mark was a good candidate. Paul was understandably unsure of Mark's reliability and didn't want the kid to join them, while Barnabas didn't see an issue with it. Their conclusion? Paul and

Barnabas parted ways and headed in opposite directions. But neither of them traveled alone, as Barnabas rolled out with Mark and Paul solicited the help of Silas. Even in the middle of a disagreement, both men knew being alone was a bad idea.

While traveling, Paul and Silas were no strangers to opposition, occasionally even finding themselves in jail. To further illustrate the need to travel two-by-two, we need to take a hard look at one of these prison sentences. After Paul and Silas go head-to-head with a fortune teller, the local government opts to toss them in jail. And it wasn't just a cell; the jailer put them in maximum security prison, complete with leg irons.

Now I don't know about you, but if my friend David and I were put in prison for evangelizing, we'd both be pretty discouraged. But not Paul and Silas. Check out what happens:

About midnight Paul and Silas were praying and singing hymns to God, and the other prisoners were listening to them. Suddenly there was such a violent earthquake that the foundations of the prison were shaken. At once all the prison doors flew open, and everybody's chains came loose.

Acts 16:25-26

Unbelievably, these two guys started to sing! Instead of sulking on the floor, they started praising God in front of the other prisoners. And since God is exactly who He says He is, the floor shook, the chains fell off, and the cell door flew open.

Here's my take on the recount of Paul and Silas being in jail and how it correlates to guys just like us living in the world today. I would imagine neither Paul nor Silas were feeling too great about their circumstances. In fact, if it were me and my friend, we would probably both be considered the "dumper" on a day like that. Two men who were traveling together watched the world cave in around both of them simultaneously. That actually sounds like a few lunches David and I have had together, where we both felt awful.

But I would submit to you one very important point. The Bible merely says Paul and Silas were praying and singing. It does not, however, mention who started singing first. One of those two guys had to be the first one to start the hymn, and the other man likely followed. If neither one had started singing, they'd still be in a sealed cell. In an authentic friendship today, no matter the condition of either person's situation, someone has to be strong enough to pull the other guy out of the pit. That's the essence of two-by-two.

In light of the church body, consider how Jesus related to His church and His disciples. We just read that Jesus sent 72 *additional* disciples out into the world in pairs. That would mean that, at the time, Jesus sent out a total of 84 men in teams of two. But of those 84, suffice it to say, there were 12 to whom Jesus was a little closer. These were the men who traveled with Jesus for three full years. They watched dead men rise, blind people see, and 5,000 men fed with little more than five biscuits and a couple of fish.

Within the confines of the 12 disciples, I have noticed there were three of them around Jesus whenever He did anything really cool. Peter, James, and John were with Jesus when He raised Jairus' daughter from the dead (*Mark 5:37*), when the Lord was transfigured (*Mark 9:2*), and when He prayed at the Garden of Gethsemane on the night prior to His crucifixion (*Mark 14:33*). By this, you could naturally assume that Jesus might have been a little tighter with those three men than He was with the other nine Disciples.

We can even drill deeper into Jesus' personal relationships with His disciples by looking at John. Countless times in the Gospel of John, John is referred to as "the one Jesus loved" or the "Beloved Disciple." Some will likely say, "Well yeah… John wrote the Gospel of John, so maybe he just had an overblown view of himself." But I want to call your attention to something to reflect how Jesus related specifically to this one man, John:

> *When Jesus saw his mother there, and the disciple whom he loved standing nearby, he said to his mother, "Dear woman, here is your son," and to the disciple, "Here is your mother." From that time on, this disciple took her into his home.*
>
> *John 19:26-27*

Call it whatever you want, but when Jesus was hanging on the cross, He very specifically assigned John the task of caring for His mother, Mary. Jesus was intentional in creating a relationship between those two people, and it was to be a lasting relationship at that.

Clearly, even Jesus possessed a very clear set of very different relationships in the context of His disciples. That can easily translate into men in the church these days:

The 72 Disciples

This would be your home church. This is the bigger body in which you play a role.

The 12 Disciples
This would be your men's ministry or small group. These are the guys you travel with at an academically deeper level than the Sunday morning experience.

The 3 Disciples
This is your accountability group. The guys you "do life" with. The ones who see you at your best and your worst.

The 1 Disciple
This is your accountability partner. No holds barred battle and love, and the guy you would trust with your wife and your wallet.

You can't go wrong if you follow the pattern Jesus did:

72-12-3-1

There are subtle differences between the three-man and one-man structures. You can visualize the purpose of three men by looking at Moses. In Exodus 17, while Joshua was battling the Amalekites, Moses was charged was holding his staff over his head. As long as Moses kept that stick over his head, Joshua was winning. But Moses grew tired, and he sought the help of Aaron and Hur. When Moses could no longer keep the staff elevated, Aaron grabbed one arm and Hur grabbed the other and literally held Moses' hands up. And when he could no longer stand, they put a rock under him so he could sit. I believe Aaron and Hur were partly responsible for the success of the Israelite army because of their willingness to be Moses' teammates.

Contrast the pragmatic and practical relationship between Moses, Aaron, and Hur to that of David and Jonathan. These guys were so tight that Jonathan actually sacrificed his relationship with his own father, King Saul, to keep David alive more than once. There was a covenant, both spoken and unspoken, that David and Jonathan would forever protect each other from harm, including caring for their respective children in the future.

So while being connected to a church body is important, significant importance can be placed on progressively deeper relationships. It took Jesus three years to build relationship with the disciples, and that involved being virtually inseparable for that duration. In fact, after all that time together, even one of the disciples, Judas, didn't make the cut.

Invest the time and pray for the right men to come alongside you as you battle life and your walk will become less brutal. It's not that you won't have challenges. We are "in the world, but not of it," and Jesus assured us we would be hammered on and persecuted as we choose to follow Him. But it's so much easier when a man supports, encourages, and keeps you "tight and right" with God as he journeys with you. It's really just a matter of shaking off our misperception of biblical manhood and yoking ourselves to other godly men, regardless of what the world may say.

Onward!

Activation Questions

- *Have I ever been involved in a men's group? Am I still? If not, why not? If so, why?*

- *Do I have a guy I could call at 3 a.m. who would pick up the phone?*

- *Who has God placed on my heart to be my Jonathan (my accountability partner)?*

8.

WAX ON, WAX OFF
(Understanding Our Role in the Church)

W e have a son, Mike, who has a unique penchant for watching the same movies over and over again. A few years ago, he was on a *Karate Kid* kick (no pun intended). Not the new version with Will Smith's kid, but the original film with "Daniel-san" and Mr. Miyagi. I recall walking past the TV to the exact same scene I had seen just hours before, and I realized Daniel Larusso was just like many men I had met serving in the local church. I know you are sitting there thinking, "Really? This I have to see." Let me unpack it for you and I swear you'll agree.

Very much against his will, Daniel Larusso is forced to move from New Jersey to Receda, California. His mother is offered a new job, and Daniel has no alternative but to go with her. Now if you've ever been forcibly uprooted because of a parent's job, especially as a teenager, Daniel's anger may just resonate with you. I recall, when I was 12 years old, being told by my father we were moving from Florida to Oregon. I was in the sixth grade, and the only thing I knew about Oregon was that it had a trail of some sort. It's an odd fraternity we're in, but there are a lot of men who were moved because of work relocations. Only those who have experienced it can truly feel Daniel's pain.

Daniel suddenly finds himself at a new school on the opposite side of the country, and the mere culture shock of moving from New Jersey to California is overwhelming. In his quest to make some new friends, Daniel attends a beach party where he encounters Ali, the girl of his dreams. And, like many teenage girls, Ali comes complete with a very egocentric ex-boyfriend named Johnny. If you recall, Johnny is not only a jerk, but he also travels in a pack with a bunch of other guys from the Cobra Kai dojo. He's a black belt in karate, and he earmarks Daniel as his new punching bag.

In the weeks following Daniel's first encounter with the Johnny, the Cobra Kai kids make the New Jersey transplant's life miserable. Around every corner, they jump him and beat on him. Fed up, Daniel plays a prank on the group, flooding a bathroom stall with water while Johnny is sitting on the toilet. A soaking wet Johnny immediately tears after Daniel, trailed by the rest of his Cobra Kai flunkies. They catch up to Daniel, pin him against a fence, and beat him to within an inch of his life. And just as Johnny is preparing to deliver a final chest kick, Mr. Miyagi flies over the fence and lays out all six Cobra Kai.

Punch drunk and nearly unconscious, Daniel makes out the faint outline of the maintenance man from his apartment complex. You see, up until this point, Mr. Miyagi (you may remember him as Arnold from *Happy Days*) is nothing more than a little old man who fixes broken sinks and makes Bonsai trees. When Daniel learns the unassuming man is really a martial arts master, he pleads with Mr. Miyagi to teach him karate. After initially objecting, the karate master agrees and asks Daniel to show up at his house the next morning.

What ensues is a training regimen that, to put it mildly, Daniel didn't really sign up for. His first training assignment is to wash and wax all of the junk cars in front of Miyagi's house. The second is to sand every square inch of wooden deck behind his home. The third is to paint all of the perimeter fences around the home. One of the funniest parts of this movie occurs during the fence-painting scene. Daniel appears to be almost done, and Mr. Miyagi walks in, carrying buckets of paint.

"Big board, right hand. Small board, left hand," he coaches.

Since only three boards remain, Daniel remarks, "But I'm almost done."

"Whole fence," says his mentor, signaling at what appears to be about 500 linear miles of wooden fence encompassing the entire yard. And, to further add to Daniel's frustration, he is met with an objection when he later reports to Mr. Miyagi that the whole fence is complete: "Both side?" asks Miyagi.

All Daniel can manage to say is, "Not yet."

The training continues with Daniel appearing early one morning to find only a note that reads: "Paint House. No up-down. Go side-side. $1/2$ left hand, $1/2$ right hand." This note is understandably Daniel's breaking point. He simply kicks the brush, mutters an obscenity, and sits down. Somehow, knowing he should finish the job in spite of his anger, Daniel paints the house anyway.

As nightfall arrives, Mr. Miyagi returns home with a fishing pole. "How come you didn't tell me you were going fishing?" the paint-covered Daniel asks. "You weren't here when I go," responds the master. After some heated banter, Mr. Miyagi drives the proverbial nail into the coffin of Daniel's training by saying, "Besides, you can't go. You karate training." If you remember this scene at all, Daniel loses his mind. He fires back, mocking the concept of karate training. "I'm what? I'm being your slave; that's what I'm being. I wax your cars, sand your deck, paint your fence for you... training, HA!" screams Daniel.

"Well, not everything is as seems," replies the calm Miyagi. Stop here and let those words permeate your mind. That statement is the lynch pin that holds this chapter together, and I promise you will never look at being a Christian man in the local church the same way again. Here's how it goes down with Daniel and Miyagi.

Daniel finally calls it quits. "I'm outta here," he mutters. But Miyagi calls the angry student back and asks him to simply show him wax on, wax off. Then he asks him to sand the deck, paint the fence, and finally paint the house. Daniel gives Miyagi a half-hearted display of his best home improvement moves, while his master corrects and occasionally rebukes him.

Then comes the real purpose of the work. Mr. Miyagi again commands, "Show me wax on, wax off," only this time, he throws a punch at Daniel's face. Suddenly, that repetitive waxing maneuver becomes a defensive posture, and Daniel deflects the punch. As it turns out, every move learned throughout the process of waxing, painting, and sanding served the dual purpose of forming muscle memory and instilling proper technique. In one final barrage, Mr. Miyagi hits Daniel with everything he has only to be deflected more than a dozen times. A stunned Daniel looks at Mr. Miyagi as his trainer simply says, "Come back tomorrow."

Now I told you the whole karate training sequence was just like most guys I know who are serving in the local church. Well, here it is:

Every week, we walk into a church on Sunday morning and hear messages about loving God, loving our wives, serving, missions, and about a million other things. One January, I remember being challenged by my pastor to read the entire New Testament in 30 days. That's an average of 11 chapters every day for a month! Sure thing! Let me just add that to my already overflowing plate.

We are also often the recipients of the tithing messages. We hear we are to sow 10% into our home church. And it's usually followed by the monthly "new building" offering or the support of one of dozens of missionaries. We get coached on prayer, hear about using our gifts for the body of Christ, and see bulletins stuffed with places where we're needed. Join the usher team, join the band, join the prayer team, but for God's sake, man, don't be a loser… just join!

And without fail, almost every month, some guy approaches us to attend the monthly men's breakfast. This is what we like to call "Saturday morning, burnt pancakes, two testimonies, and a prayer." It's a combination of food, a quick devotional, and a story or two. It kills the first two hours of our Saturday, and the impact is often nominal at best. Guys who meet once a month aren't going to be too transparent. Only the diehard church dudes show up, and the prayers usually revolve around someone's aunt in New York who has a dog with cataracts or something like that. But we go mostly to avoid being accosted by this guy at the urinals in the bathroom. Let's face it, men, we get asked to do a lot of stuff in the church.

As if that isn't enough, we also have our friends and church mates monitoring our every move. We have to make absolutely sure our halo is never crooked in front of any of our brothers at church. Our unchurched friends are watching us like a hawk from the sidelines, too, in the hope of catching us in some sort of life-altering hypocrisy just so they can discredit not only us but also our Savior. And just like Mr. Miyagi, we have buddies who go fishing on Sunday morning while we are cooling our heels, or so it appears, in church. We can't win.

To add insult to injury, not only do we have to follow the instructions of our pastor, serve in the church, and make sure we always appear perfect in front of other people, but then throw in what the Bible asks us to do as we strive to be like Jesus, or Paul, or any one of those men we read about. I'm already wiped out just writing about this stuff, and it's exponentially more difficult keeping all of these balls in the air without dropping one in real life.

In no particular order, the Bible encourages us to read the Word, meditate on it, pray, fast, serve others, put everyone's needs ahead of our own, love our wives sacrificially, discipline our children, and take care of widows and orphans. I'm just thankful Jesus came to live among us, if only to eradicate all of the animal sacrifices and altar offerings spelled out in Leviticus. We men are already overloaded. It sure seems like a lot of wax on, wax off; sand the floor; paint the fence stuff, doesn't it?

But not everything is as it seems. Whether it's teaching Sunday school or helping with the youth car wash fundraiser, whether it's a quiet time regimen or a message about sacrifice, all of the seemingly unrelated things we are asked to do by the church, and by God Himself, are designed to create a balanced and deadly warrior for Christ.

Just like Daniel Larusso, if you have grown tired of all of the busy work you associate with church life, it's time to see the tasks for what they really are. We were called, perhaps even before we were born, to conquer superhuman tasks for the kingdom of God:

"For we are God's workmanship, created in Christ Jesus to do good works, which God prepared in advance for us to do."

Ephesians 2:10

In essence, according to the writer of Ephesians, we are the craftsmanship of a Holy God, and we were saved by grace through Jesus Christ to perform incredible feats for Him. And the verse goes on to tell us that God already put the game plan together before we even reported for duty. In other words, God knew we would be star quarterbacks on His team before we even showed up for practice. So on the outside, what appears to be running the same plays over and over in the summer heat are really the tactical drills needed to get us ready for game day.

There are recounts of men in the Bible who appeared to be spinning their wheels when they were, in fact, being readied to be warriors. These men were like race horses, trapped in the starting gate waiting to run, but God didn't let them run without some heavy preparation.

In Genesis, Joseph was burned by his own blood brothers and consequently spent 15 years as a slave. Even when he was rescued, he wound up in jail and was again forgotten, by a friend no less, only to spend another two years in an Egyptian prison cell. But after 17 grueling years of preparation, he became the Pharaoh's right-hand man and ultimately saved the entire nation of Israel from starvation during a deadly famine.

King David was to be anointed the king of Israel, but before he could put on the crown and take his rightful spot on the throne, he first had to dodge flying spears and countless threats on his life by none other than his predecessor, King Saul. David started out as a musician for Saul and soon became a hero after felling the giant Philistine, Goliath, with a pebble and a slingshot. Years later, he spent his valuable time hiding from Saul in caves, fearing for his life. King David eventually became the greatest king to reign over God's chosen people, but it took some serious cave preparation to get there.

Before he scribed the vast majority of the New Testament, and before becoming the apostle to the Gentiles, Saul of Tarsus (aka, the apostle Paul) had to be blinded and knocked off of his high horse (literally) to answer the call. And even after his supernatural call into ministry, Paul was, without a doubt, the most abused disciple of all:

> *"I have worked much harder, been in prison more frequently, been flogged more severely, and been exposed to death again and again. Five times I received from the Jews the forty lashes minus one. Three times I was beaten with rods, once I was pelted with stones, three times I was shipwrecked, I spent a night and a day in the open sea, I have been constantly on the move. I have been in danger from rivers, in danger from bandits, in danger from my fellow Jews, in danger from Gentiles; in danger in the city, in danger in the country, in danger at sea; and in danger from false believers. I have labored and toiled and have often gone without sleep; I have known hunger and thirst and have often gone without food; I have been cold and naked. Besides everything else, I face daily the pressure of my concern for all the churches."*

> *2 Corinthians 11:23b-28*

Suddenly, neither my "suffering" for the cause of Christ nor my sacrifice during preparation seem nearly as bad when lined up next to Paul. There is so much truth to the statement "when you start feeling bad about yourself, just remember somebody else always has it worse."

In some respects, the apostle Peter faced the most stringent preparation of all. When Jesus was on trial before the Sanhedrin, Peter denied he even knew Jesus three different times. What's even more astounding is Jesus had predicted it. So after Peter hears the rooster crow, indicating that he had just been busted doing precisely what his Lord had cautioned he would, he had to feel terrible.

It's no secret that Jesus rose from the dead three days after His burial, just as He said would happen. Peter knew this, and my guess is he was a little stressed out when Jesus showed up again. After all, the last time Peter had any interaction with Jesus, he had turned his back on Him three times. Fortunately for Peter, he was also obviously specifically earmarked to do something incredible, because Jesus called him out before He even appeared to His disciples. Immediately after Jesus' resurrection, Mary Magdelene and her friends encountered an open tomb and an angel dressed in white. The angel informed Mary that Jesus was no longer in the tomb and then urged her:

"But go, tell his disciples and Peter, 'He is going ahead of you into Galilee. There you will see him, just as he told you.'"

Mark 16:7

Color me nuts, but wasn't Peter a disciple? So why did the angel mention him separately? My guess is that his disciple card had been revoked, and Jesus had to work through some issues with Peter before he was reinstated, so to speak. We learn later, in John 21, that Jesus had a couple of questions for Peter, three to be exact. "Peter, do you love me?" was the threefold question, and three times Peter was compelled to answer with a resounding "yes." Peter's previous denials warranted an equal, but opposite, answer. Three denials required three "I love you's."

As was the original plan of the Lord, Peter became the rock on which Christ built His church. He was literally the first official pastor. That was a monumental calling that required a whole lot of "wax on, wax off" to get there.

So the next time you think you are just counting widgets and wasting your time, remember that preparation, as with any form of practice or discipline, may seem oddly disconnected and pretty worthless. If you've done any time in the military, you may have even questioned the reasoning behind some of the commands you were given. I think Colonel Nathan Jessup from *A Few Good Men* says it best: *"We follow orders or people die."*

If you look at your personal "wax on, wax off" as basic training for the battle of life and view yourself as a combat ready soldier waiting to be deployed, then all of the mundane tasks will interlock to make you into the defender of your wife, your children and your God.

Oh, and in case you were wondering, I really did read the New Testament in 30 days after my pastor challenged us.

Now we just have to figure out why we often refuse to grab the car wax, the sandpaper, or the paintbrush.

Activation Questions

- *Have I ever been a part of a church? What was I asked to do?*

- *Have I ever permanently left a church frustrated? Why?*

- *Do I ever feel like all of the things I do for God and the church have no meaning?*

- *Looking at all of the circumstantial evidence (church life, home life and work life), what mission do I think God has prepared for me to do?*

9.

ANOTHER FOUR LETTER "F-WORD"
(Why We Won't Engage with Other Guys)

Now before you get all offended, let me assure you that this chapter is not what you think it is. But I think it's important to understand why most of us men don't have any friends and, frankly, don't really want any. You married guys are going to get this one right out of the gate.

If I detect something is amiss with my wife, and I nonchalantly ask her, "What's wrong?" I will likely get one of several answers. She may actually tell me exactly what is on her mind, especially if it has nothing to do with me. Or she may unload on me about what I just said, did, or acted like that completely irritated her. Or I may get the phrase that every husband dreads: "I'm *fine*." If you are like me, you know right away that if she says she's fine, you can be certain she's anything but. It's the ultimate four-letter F-word, and we men know what it means. Grab a pillow or a shovel, because we are either sleeping on the couch or digging our way out of it.

The word "fine" has also become one of the best ways to repel the question "how are you?" Most of the time, things aren't fine, but we men have figured out "fine" is a very effective man repellent. With women, the word means "I'm really mad at you and don't want to talk about it." With men, it means "get out of my face. I don't know you that well, nor do I particularly trust you."

Look at it this way. Remember Mr. Potato Head? He was a plastic toy with holes in his head for different eyes, mouths, and shoes. You older guys may even remember using a real potato, but the updated model came fully equipped with various facial features stored in a trunk in his butt. When we see a man approaching us at church, we reach into our butt-trunk and pull out our best smile and slide it over our real countenance. I call this the "Mr. Potato Head smile," and we're really proficient at switching our facial features to avoid undue questioning.

So exactly how did this become our first line of defense? I mean, how can we expect anyone to pray for us or help us if we don't shoot straight? I have narrowed it down to one word: "trust." We don't trust anyone, and it's really no wonder, given how often we get burned or let down by other guys, both in the world and in the church.

The world tells us to be "self-made men" or to "pull yourself up by the bootstraps." There are dozens of phrases that lead us to being isolated, self-insufficient, and completely untrusting. I spent quite a few years working in the marketplace prior to embarking into ministry, and one lesson I learned was "don't trust anyone." It seemed as if everyone, including my own key employees, were after my job, my company car and my paycheck. Knowing this, I spent the vast majority of my time allowing no one into my personal space. And whether I was asked how the division was performing or how I was feeling, the answer was always "fine."

The church is another arena where "I'm fine" works to stave off an imminent personal space invasion. After all, they don't usually care how we're doing anyway, right? It's just an ice-breaker of sorts. Can you imagine if we really answered the question "how are you?" with the truth? In a lot of cases, people would break into a dead run in the opposite direction. So why have we become so untrusting in the church, too? Isn't the church supposed to be a safe place full of trainwrecks just like us?

Like a lot of men, I wasn't raised in the church. In fact, my dad was pretty much agnostic, and my mother was raised Mormon. And like a lot of men, it took a significant loss for me to look for God. I recall being a senior in high school when a close classmate of mine passed away. He had contracted pneumonia, and all points indicated that he would be released on Monday. In what appeared to be out of nowhere, he died over the weekend. Crushed and confused, I sought out some of those "Christian kids." Even a veteran heathen like me knew those Jesus kids were the right people to pursue. I started hanging out with them and even got connected with their youth group.

In world of aviation, a "near miss" is when two planes pass on the same horizontal plane within 500 feet of one another but don't collide. I guess you could say the death of my friend was a near miss with the Lord, primarily because almost every one of my Christian support mechanisms fell away mere months after the funeral. And after seeing some of the kids drinking at the same parties, the seeds of hypocrisy were sown. And I quickly abandoned God.

But my journey to avoid the Lord actually stemmed from an event in my life that occurred when I was only nine years old. I was invited to an all-you-can-eat hotdog feed at a local Baptist church by one of my friends, and I was stoked! You see, my mother was a bit of a food monitor, and the words "all-you-can-eat" were not in her vocabulary. She was one of those moms who replied with, "Just wait until your brain catches up to your stomach," when I said, "I'm still hungry." I was floored she gave me permission, so I set out to put Oscar Mayer out of business.

I walked into the church life center and took my seat with 100 or so other "'tweens." Needless to say, with the metal chairs and metal tables on the old school asbestos flooring, it was a little loud. Over my shoulder, a nice lady set a paper plate in front of me loaded with a hot dog, potato chips, and Kool-Aid. As I settled in for the long haul, telling the lady to just run a tab and keep 'em coming, this frightening old guy (he must have been at least 30) came up and inquired, "You don't go to church here, do you, son?"

"No sir," I replied.

"Do you know Jesus?" he asked.

I have to be honest that, at this point in my life, the only thing I knew about Jesus was the five-minute recap of Luke 2 that Linus gives in that *A Charlie Brown Christmas* movie. "No, I don't," I replied to the scary dude.

The man simply said, "Come with me for a minute." Being my elder, I quickly obeyed and followed him into a small room with several other kids my age. The man proceeded to inform me that, since I didn't know who Jesus was, my mother, father, sister, and I were all going to hell. I sobbed all the way home, having only eating half of my hot dog, and then my mother got involved. Suffice it to say, the pastor of that church knew how my mom felt and was likely sent to Siberia to finish out his call.

As a result of the hot dog shock, when my wife suggested, decades later, that we attend our local Baptist church, I panicked. There was no way that was happening, because when I heard the word "Baptist," all I could think of was hot dogs and hell.

You may be that guy who has been burned by somebody in a church. I have heard it said that church would be a lot better if we could just get rid of all of the people. I am here to tell you that you aren't alone, and it's time to get back in the game. We need to be connected to the body through a local church, and regardless of what happened in the past, God needs us utilizing our very specific gifts in His church.

On the other hand, maybe you've been connected in the church and you fell prey to what I call "prayer gossip." There's a really fine line between the two, which you may have discovered. Some people just LOVE to talk about other people, and some church folks have found a way to combine the two by spiritualizing gossip.

It happens all the time. A man (let's call him "Jim") confesses a pornography addiction which, by the way, is an epidemic among men, whether in or out of the church. The guy finally has the stones to tell the men in his accountability group, and they commit to banding together to help. Unfortunately for Jim, one of the men in his group has to go to his couple's small group that night. When the official call for prayer requests comes up, Jim's buddy stands up and says, "We really need to pray for Jim. He has a bit of a computer problem, if you know what I mean." The gossip wheel spins, and Jim gets stared at by everyone the following Sunday. After all of that, do you think Jim will ever share anything with anyone again?

At some point, many of us get burned by a church person. My counsel to you is "Don't throw the baby out with the bath water." Make sure there is confidence in your accountability group, as that is rule number one. If you aren't feeling it with a particular bunch of guys, seek excellence elsewhere, but don't abandon groups. The enemy would like nothing better than to get you off by yourself to battle alone. Ecclesiastes 4:10 says, "Pity the man who falls and has no one to pick him up." Don't go it alone. Remember Maverick?

Perhaps the guy who was pivotal in keeping me away from the kingdom for decades and didn't realize it was a former coworker of mine named Bruce. Bruce was a born-again believer, and at the time, I was an out-of-control drinker. There were days when I would report to work almost directly from the bar, and as I worked with Bruce, I began to ask some serious questions. I knew there had to be more to life than partying, and I was stuck with Bruce all day long. Like any seeker, I inquired about God, Christianity, the validity of Scripture, and whatever else popped into my pickled brain. Then the topic of women and sex came up; I knew Christians had a different view about it than I did at the time. Bruce simply stated he and his wife believed sex was designed for procreation. "My wife and I are done having kids," he beamed proudly, "so I haven't touched my wife in a decade." And thus ended my pursuit of Christianity yet again.

Newsflash! Some of us Christians can be pretty "out there." We are legalistic, judgmental, and even downright mean sometimes. But there are also some real Jesus lovers out there who love like He does. On behalf of Christian men everywhere, I would like to apologize if you have been accosted by a crazy person.

No matter the reason, God wants us off the bench and on the field. Whether you have been gossiped about, had your trust violated, or had a near miss or two with Jesus, God loves you and needs you yoked with some other guys in the battle for our lives and our wives. Time is short, and men need other men. So walk it off and get back in the game.

Activation Questions

- *In the world, who do I trust implicitly?*

- *Have I ever had my confidence violated by a Christian?*

- *How did I respond when I discovered the breach of confidentiality?*

- *Has a previously bad experience with a Christian kept me from engaging?*

- *How can I shake off the past hurt and re-engage?*

10

SUPERFICIAL
(My Problem isn't Contagious, Dude)

Another great source of mass casualties in Christendom is the all-too-prevalent faker. You may have met him before in the church or even at work. He smiles, knows all the right things to say, and even plugs in the occasional "praise God" for good measure. He says he will be there for you when times get difficult; but when the going gets tough, he gets gone.

A young man walks into the law offices of Joe Miller, a small-time attorney in the city of Philadelphia. Miller appears to be more like a shyster than an actual lawyer, and this young man, Andrew Beckett, has seen Miller's cheesy TV commercial and is there for urgent legal help.

It's the mid-1980s, and Andrew has just been fired from his longtime career—as an attorney, of all things. Up until a few days ago, Beckett was a key player at a large, conservative Philadelphia law firm. He was the rising star. The starting QB. He was the guy whose number got called for the big cases. And he was summarily fired out of nowhere.

You probably recognize this storyline as the one from the movie *Philadelphia*, which stars Tom Hanks as Beckett and Denzel Washington as his not-so-polished attorney. Beckett was indeed fired, and it was cited by his firm that it was performance-based. But it was, in fact, due to the young man's diagnosis with the then relatively unknown disease called AIDS.

His firm wanted nothing to do with Andrew's lifestyle or his illness, so they released him as quickly as possible.

So now Beckett finds himself in Miller's office with zero options. As they meet and exchange pleasantries, it appears to be the convergence of two legal minds. Beckett gives Miller the backstory and then discloses the real reason for his sudden termination from the firm. Miller, visibly shaken at the word "AIDS," states, "Sorry, but I just don't see a case, counselor." After the HIV bomb detonates, Miller is pretty quick to get Beckett out of his office and so calls an end to the meeting.

And what does Miller do the minute Andrew Beckett is gone? He sanitizes his whole office… the stapler, the chair, and anything else the sick man has touched. Then he gets on the phone for an immediate doctor's appointment to confirm that he, too, has not been infected with AIDS. It's really sort of comical considering we now know that HIV can never be transmitted through a Swingline.

Let's take the same scenario and move it into our community of men, both in and out of the church. Not the AIDS part, but Miller's reaction to it. We get together with other men, we sharpen each other, and we pray for each other. At church, we greet men and we really want them to be a part of what God is doing.

However, the minute a man in our group says he is battling pornography, is having an affair, has lost his job, or is in the throes of an unrecoverable marital flatspin, something happens to us. We often back away, as if there is some way we are going to catch it. Just like Joe Miller's fear of contracting AIDS from a doorknob, we pull back, sanitize ourselves, and often go "superficial" on the man. At the very moment when he needs us the most, we freak out and bail on him.

You know, Jesus made a point of hanging out with the people you and I would be the most likely to run from. Lepers, sick people, losers, rejects... and He loved them. When talking about why He ate with sinners and tax collectors instead of the churchy Pharisee types, He said:

"It is not the healthy who need a doctor, but the sick. I have not come to call the righteous, but sinners."

Mark 2:17

When Jesus was on his way to heal the ailing daughter of Jairus, He stopped dead in His tracks when a bleeding woman touched the hem of His garment:

Then the woman, seeing that she could not go unnoticed, came trembling and fell at his feet. In the presence of all the people, she told why she had touched him and how she had been instantly healed. Then he said to her, "Daughter, your faith has healed you. Go in peace."

Luke 8:47-48

And, believe it or not, while Jesus was busy healing the sick woman, Jairus' daughter died. Our Savior never acted as if He was ever bothered, and He raised Jairus' little girl from the dead. And in spite being both fully God and fully man, He never concerned Himself with worrying about catching anything. He just loved everyone. He healed blind guys, lepers, and paralytics.

Even when it came to matters of sin, which are obviously not contagious, Jesus loved people through their battles. There was a woman who had committed adultery, and the whole town was ready to stone her to death when Jesus interceded. After pointing out that even the purest human still had sin, the angry crowd disbanded, leaving only Jesus and the woman sitting in the dirt. And what did Jesus do?

> *Jesus straightened up and asked her, "Woman, where are they? Has no one condemned you?" "No one, sir," she said, "Then neither do I condemn you," Jesus declared. "Go now and leave your life of sin."*
>
> *John 8:10-11*

Jesus knew she was as guilty as the day was long, but He didn't condemn her. He spoke kindly and was the last one to leave. It really didn't matter if a person was physically ill or just a societal trainwreck; Jesus cared about them all.

So the next time a close friend tells you that his wife is leaving him, don't chase the guy out of your office. Divorce isn't contagious, addiction can't be spread by a handshake, and I promise he won't sneeze his cancer all over you. Love like Jesus and walk these guys through their pain.

Remember:

> *"I tell you the truth, whatever you did for one of the least of these brothers of mine, you did for me."*
>
> *Matthew 25:40*

Don't disconnect because of what may have happened to you. And remember to treat every man just like Jesus treats you, no matter what.

In the next chapters, we're going to dig into some maladies that plague us as men. Lots of us.

Activation Questions

- *Has anyone ever stopped talking to me because I told them about my personal struggles?*

- *Is how I was treated acting as a roadblock to trusting anyone?*

- *What would I do if a man in my men's group announced he had contracted AIDS?*

- *Have I ever reacted to someone like a Pharisee instead of like Jesus? What would I do differently now?*

11

SO WHAT'S YOUR STORY, BRO?
(We Become What We Hear)

E very man has a story. And you're thinking, "Yeah, man... I know this already." You may be recalling that point in your life when God rescued you. You can regale other Christian men with the tale of a life transformed by the power of Jesus and stand pretty much toe-to-toe with anyone else's testimony of salvation. And that's exactly what that is: your testimony.

Every man has a testimony, but that isn't the "story" to which I'm referring in this case. Our "story" is a foundational belief system of who we are based on the interactions we have had and the words we've heard from other people. It's one of the defining characteristics of how we view ourselves every day. And it's usually just a big, fat lie. You see, our story is really more like a parallel universe or a terrible B-grade movie that has become the framework of how we see who we are. We re-read that story every time we encounter someone or even look in the mirror. Even worse, we find new ways to confirm this alternate reality all the time.

In most cases, the first words penned into our "story" come from our fathers, since they are usually the first men who begin to shape who we are as men. Let me explain.

I remember being a kid of about seven or eight years old. I lived in Jacksonville, Florida at the time, and my mom had this 1963 Dodge Dart. You "car guys" may remember this vehicular masterpiece, with its Slant-6 motor and pushbutton transmission (seriously… you pushed "D" for drive on the dashboard). My mom's Dart was white, and I vividly recall the paint was falling off. It really looked more like a stick of chalk than a car simply to due to a decade of car wax negligence. It was a sunny day, and I had a buddy over. I was given a simple enough task; my father asked me to run out to the driveway and get the keys my mother had inadvertently left in the Dart's ignition.

So I bounded out to mom's car to grab the keys. Now the only thing I had ever seen anyone do with keys in an ignition was what? Yeah, I turned them. I freaked out, my friend cheered, and my dad came blazing out of the back door and yanked me out of the car. He swatted my butt hard and accused me of showing off, and I cowered away in tears from the embarrassment of it all happening in front of my friend. You know, it really was an accident, and I think my dad finally believed me when I reiterated that fact when I was in my thirties. After all, who defends a lie for three decades? It really was an honest mistake.

I began to write a story about myself on that day. It simply read, "I can't do anything right." Many men have written this story about themselves, and it gets confirmed time and time again. In my case, it was in high school. I was a really good student for the most part, and it wasn't uncommon to have a report card with all A's and one B on it. And the B was usually for PE, so it wasn't like it was a real grade anyway, right? I would bring my report card home and hand it to my dad. Like a lot of dads, myself included, he tended to make a lot of non-verbal grunting noises when he read over the top of his glasses. Report cards were no exception. After a series of "Hmms" and sighs, he would take off his glasses and, using the earpiece, would point at the lone B and ask, "What happened here?"

Really? I bring home a report card with all A's and one B and the B becomes the topic of discussion? Whether it was intentional or not, do you know what this told me? You guessed it. "I can't do anything right." And my "story" was validated yet again.

Do you see how it works? We actually LOOK for ways to solidify a bad story in concrete. And then, to make matters worse, it translates into our adult life.

I get literally hundreds of e-mails every week. Most of them are positive, edifying tales of a life changed through the live *Rough Cut Men* Movie Experience events. But every so often, I get the guy who disagrees with something I said, or a movie clip I used to illustrate a point. One man in particular hammered on me about using an R-rated movie, *Saving Private Ryan*. Bear in mind that the clip is edited for content and language and could actually be shown in a kindergarten class, but this guy decided to not only assault the clip but also opted to assassinate my character, speaking ability, and maybe even my mother by the time he was done. It killed me. I kept that e-mail in my Inbox and re-read it a dozen times. I forwarded it to my wife, who told me to just blow it off. But it hurt. And, in spite of hundreds of e-mails to the contrary, this brutal e-mail haunted me for weeks. And you know what it told me? "I can't do anything right." Even as an adult, I confirmed my "story" again.

My story has even reared its ugly head in my marriage. My wife, Joni, is what I call a "drive-by" wife. She thinks on her feet… and she thinks fast! She has wanted coach lights installed by our garage for a while now. Actually, it's been eight years, but I'll get to it . My home office is actually our living room, and I am usually up to my ears in managing both an international ministry and a family of seven, so I'm typically deep in thought when she comes home from the store. She will set the groceries down, and since she has just walked past the two gaping holes where those coach lights should be, she will quickly state, "We really need those coach lights." Exasperated, I just sigh. After all, I really do want to get to those lights, but I never seem to be able to get to the bottom of my "to-do" list long enough to do it. I'm a guy, and I want to be a great husband like every other man, and I work hard to cover all the bases. And although she means no harm by it, the coach lights again confirm that no matter how much I do right, I still don't do it all. I quietly tell myself, "See? You can't do anything right."

By now, I'm probably telling a similar tale to some of the men reading this book. We buy a bad story, watch it over and over again, and it becomes a defining point of who we are. And again, it's a lie.

How do you defeat a bad "story"? It's easier than you think. You simply replace it with the Truth. What does God say about who I am? He says I am *"fearfully and wonderfully made" (Ps. 131:14).* I'm the apple of His eye. He knew me before I was even born. There can't be two truths. I'm either a failure or I'm who God says I am.

I live in Sarasota, Florida, which is the home of the Ringling Brothers circus. Many of my friends are circus people. This concept of believing two truths can be best illustrated by thinking of one circus act in particular. Have you ever seen that guy who stands up between two horses and rides around the ring with a foot on each horse? Have you ever wondered what would happen if the horses decided to take off in opposite directions? Either the rider would opt for a serious groin injury, or he'd pick a horse to stand on. Choosing between a bad story and the truth of God is a lot like picking a horse. You can't continue to stand on both, right?

I encounter men all the time who have been abandoned by their fathers. My dad's dad left him when he was nine years old, for example. The moment a father walks away from his son, the son begins to pen the story "I'm not worth sticking around for" or—worse yet—"I'm unlovable." We don't know the mitigating circumstances about why Dad left, but the story is still written in the mind of the abandoned young man.

Going forward, that single action by Dad will resonate like a gunshot in other relationships. The abandoned young man finds himself married, and because of the "I'm unlovable" story, he tends to do one of two things. He either clutches on to his wife for dear life, suffocating her emotionally. Or he pushes her away, fearful that committing his heart will again result in hurt. So he stays at arm's length, so to speak. Do you know what happens when a man holds on too tightly or never engages emotionally? Often, it becomes self-fulfilling prophecy and his wife leaves. And the man simply says, "You see? I told you I wasn't worth sticking around for." And the bad story is confirmed.

This same guy will also often become a workaholic in order to hold on to a job. If an unfortunate downsizing occurs or the company folds up shop, you can probably imagine this man again has a way to confirm his story. "You see," he says, "I'm unlovable."

As I mentioned a few paragraphs ago, the trick to killing a bad story is to replace it with the Word of God. Two different stories can't both be true. It can't be both "up" and "down," and it can't be both "black" and "white"… it's one or the other.

If your story is "everybody leaves me," remember that God says, *"I will never leave you nor forsake you" (Deut. 31:6).* By the way, "never" means never!

If your story is "I am nothing," remember that God says you are *"fearfully and wonderfully made" (Ps. 131:14).* Quit telling God He did a bad job assembling you! Jesus tells us just how <u>not</u> "nothing" you are:

> *"Are not two sparrows sold for a penny? Yet not one of them will fall to the ground apart from the will of your Father. And even the very hairs of your head are all numbered. So don't be afraid; you are worth more than many sparrows"*
>
> *Matthew 10:29-31*

So don't buy the lie that you are worthless, brother. Just because you may have heard these words from an earthly father, remember you are the apple of God's eye!

Perhaps you never heard the words "I love you" from your father. In John 15, Jesus says, *"I love you with an everlasting love. Always remain in my love"*

Or maybe you wake up every morning with a negative outlook on life. Dad said, "You're never going to amount to anything," and it became your "story." Replace it with what the Bible says in Jeremiah 29:11, *"For I know the plans I have for you. Plans to prosper you and not to harm you. Plans to give you a hope and a future"*

Choose today to begin to believe that the plans God has for you are plans of victory, not defeat. Regardless of what Dad said, God says "hope" and "future." Bank on it.

And if your story is like mine, "I can't do anything right," take a look at what God says: *"I can do all things through Christ who strengthens me" (Phil 4:13)*

If you don't like the "story" you've been telling yourself, then turn down the worldly noise and listen to the Lord. And just *"cast all your anxiety on him because he cares for you" (1 Peter 5:7)*

Words have a very long shelf life. This isn't the last time you will read that statement. The words we have heard from other people have drafted a story in our lives that aren't the reality of God. And these words can stick around for a lifetime if we don't replace them.

The next few chapters are all about dads in film. See if you can find your father, and perhaps your story, in there somewhere.

Activation Questions

- *Off the top of your head, list your three biggest memories from your childhood. Write them down. (Often, trauma or events are in the top three.)*

- *What "story" could you write about yourself from the three memories on your list? I shared my Dodge Dart story and the report card as an example. Random memories do tell a story.*

- *What's your story? In light of your story, what does God say about you?*

12

CHASING YOUR STUPID DREAM...
(Abandoned by Dad)

One of the most debilitating and painful epidemics coursing through the lives of men today is what is often dubbed "the father wound." Essentially, this emotional (and sometimes even physical) wounding can be best described as something Dad said (or didn't say) or did (or didn't do) that has somehow impacted how we view ourselves. In some cases, the father wound can even radically amend the direction of our lives, resulting in a completely different outcome than had the trauma never occurred.

Addressing the father wound has become a staple in the arsenal of many men's speakers and men's books over the past few decades. It's a very real problem that plagues almost every guy you meet. But I intend on taking the Father Wound to a deeper level by looking beyond the son (that would be us) and digging into the emotional history of the father (that would be our dad). Suffice it to say, if we understand where our dad came from and perhaps even view him as just another guy, we may be able to overcome our own wounding. Here's a statement that can change the way you view father wounds:

Behind every father wound, you will find a wounded father.

And there is no better way to illustrate this than through the use of some really famous Hollywood biographical movies (and one Pixar movie, just to shake things up). The next chapters are going to hit our dads head on, and their dads, and maybe even their dads, too.

In the annals of college football superstardom, you would be hard-pressed to call Daniel Ruettiger a "standout" player. A man most commonly known as "Rudy" also has a movie by the same name, which stars Sean Astin along with actors like Vince Vaughn (did you know he was in this movie?) and Jon Favreau (also the director of *Iron Man*) and veteran actors like Ned Beatty and Robert Prosky. I call this particular film a "guy cry" movie because you will absolutely shed tears at the end of the movie. Blame it on allergies if you have to.

Rudy hails from Joliet, Illinois, and comes from a very long line of steel workers. In fact, there are several non-negotiables if one happens to be a man in the Ruettiger clan. First, there is only one college football team—the Notre Dame Fighting Irish. If you're a Ruettiger, you bleed blue and gold. Secondly, Ruettiger men graduate from high school and go on to work in the local foundry. So for Rudy the die is already cast, so to speak.

But this young man has a dream, a dream that makes him the butt of a lot of family jokes. You see, Rudy wants to play football for Notre Dame. You may recall the challenges with achieving this particular dream, as he isn't exactly football player material. As one of his mentors in the movie puts it, he's "five foot nothing, a hundred and nothing, and you have barely a speck of athletic ability." Not only does he lack the physical prowess to play Division I college football, but he also doesn't have the grades to get into the university in the first place. In fact, his grades at Joliet Catholic High School are so bad that they won't even let him take a bus tour of the campus. Suffice it to say, the cards are stacked against Rudy.

Although he did play football in high school and is often recognized for the amount of heart he put into every game, Rudy doesn't move on to college but instead adheres to the Ruettiger post-high school life plan. You almost have to feel bad for the guy. Within two years, he has a job at the foundry and a fiancé who is already looking for homes in good school districts. The poor kid is a passenger on a speeding train, and his football fantasy is all but a distant memory.

There is, however, one small ember still burning in Rudy's dream. His best friend, Pete, absolutely refuses to allow Rudy's dream to die and even buys him an old Notre Dame jacket at a thrift store. During a birthday lunch in the foundry break room, Pete reminds his friend, "Having dreams is what makes life tolerable."

Tragically, Pete dies in an accident at the foundry, leaving Rudy heartbroken and somewhat directionless. During the *Rough Cut Men* Movie Experience live event, we use a clip from *Rudy* that truly reflects the lives of so many men I meet along the way. It sets up like this:

Immediately following Pete's funeral mass, Rudy makes a life-altering decision: "I'm going to South Bend," he informs his fiancé. Needless to say, with her "happy family" plans thwarted, she simply tells Rudy he will have to go it alone. He agrees, packs a duffel bag, grabs the money from his savings account, and heads to the bus station.

The subsequent scene begins very simply, with Rudy sitting on a bench in front of the Greyhound bus depot. His father appears and says, in my opinion, perhaps some of the most idiotic things a dad could say to his son. But, as with any of us who are dads ourselves, I believe Rudy's father feels his counsel to his son is solid. I call this guy the "dream killer" dad:

> "Your grandfather saved all of his life to bring the family to this country. He got a good job in the stockyards. He had a nice little house in South Chicago. I was about 12. Somebody sold him on the idea he ought to move to the country and become a dairy farmer. Well, he buys some land and gets a couple hundred cows. Within five months, every one of those cows was dead with disease. It was the Depression. He couldn't sell the land. There was no work. So one day, he took off. Didn't come back. Me and my brothers was split up to live with friends and relatives. Chasing your stupid dream causes nothing but you and everyone around you heartache. Notre Dame is for rich kids, smart kids, great athletes. It's not for us. You're a Ruettiger! There's nothing in the world wrong with being a Ruettiger. You can live a nice life. Frank is gonna take over plant number two. A couple years, he'll make more than me and Johnny. He's in charge of the expansion program."

"Notre Dame is for rich kids. Smart kids. Great athletes." What did this guy just say to his kid? "We're broke, you're as dumb as a box of rocks, and you are a terrible athlete." Then Rudy's father goes on to say chasing the dream of playing ball for the Irish was just going to end in tragedy. Then comes the kicker. His dad points him right back in the direction of the Ruettiger family legacy, a legacy of no college degree and a life predestined to the steel industry. For all intents and purposes, Rudy is pigeonholed into the mold of his father and his brothers. But even after an appeal by his father, Rudy strikes out with a bus ticket in hand and no college acceptance letter or even a place to stay.

For years, I have pointed out how terrible we should feel for poor Rudy. After all, his father literally crushed his dream at the Greyhound station. But why was his dad so determined to squash his Notre Dame vision? What could motivate an otherwise solid, at least on the surface, father to pull the plug on what his son has wanted since birth?

The answer lies in the same bus bench pep talk. Buried in the mire of bad counsel lies the truth about who Rudy's dad really is. And, countless times as I have engaged with men at live events, I hear the same dream-killer dad tale. Words like "you're never going to amount to anything" or "you will always be what you are—unsuccessful." You can see the heartbreak in these sons' eyes as they recount stories of their own dads and their failure to back them up or even believe in them.

Notice this statement: "So one day, he took off. My brothers and me was split up to live with friends and relatives." Rudy's father is riddled with emotional bullet holes because his father gave up a good job to take a chance as a farmer and it backfired, in more ways than one. First, the cows bought the farm—okay, that one was pretty bad—the cows died. His whole cattle investment became beef jerky because of the Depression, and the man simply took off. Rudy's grandfather abandoned his family, and that one relational gunshot that went off in the 1930s was still echoing in the ears of Rudy's dad some 40 years later. Obviously devastated, Rudy's father was merely living out his own nightmare right in the middle of Rudy's dream. So while it's probably okay to feel sorry for Rudy after getting hammered on a bus bench, it should break our hearts as men that his father was so wounded that the paralysis was being passed down to Rudy.

I believe Rudy's dad wrote a story when his father left the farm: "Chasing a dream equals abandonment." Rudy's grandfather chased the cow dream, and Mr. Ruettiger ended up abandoned. You know, when the boys graduated from high school in their family, they all lived within a few blocks of each other. The whole family would gather on Saturday at Rudy's dad's home and watch Notre Dame. When Rudy decided to chase his dream, and his father was diligently attempting to talk him out of it, Rudy was unknowingly writing a continuation of his father's story. First, Mr. Ruettiger's dad had chased a dream and left. And this time, Rudy was "abandoning" his father to leave town and play football. In Mr. Ruettiger's mind, both his father and now his son were leaving him.

Men, no matter what, we must get behind our kids when they have a dream. In both the Old Testament and the New Testament, God is clear in His Word to us:

"I can do everything through him who gives me strength."

Phillipians 4:13

"Is anything too hard for the LORD?"

Genesis 18:14a

The minute we hamstring our children with the legacy of what it means to be a [Insert your last name here], we may inadvertently undermine the very mission God has set before them.

And if you are one of those men who has been shackled to a family legacy you didn't build or didn't really wish to be a part of, remember your dad only modeled what he knew. Hanging onto the bitterness about what your dad said or did only impacts your forward momentum. If you woke up this morning, then God still has something for you to do. There isn't enough air on this planet for the Lord to just waste it, so it just may be time to pursue that dream after all. Regardless of what people say about the attainability of your vision, always keep in mind that God owns the cattle on a thousand hills (Psalm 50:10), and all we really need to get the job done is a T-bone steak. He has the resources, but He needs you to shake off the past and convince yourself that you are not destined to be like the guy before you. Rudy didn't.

Daniel "Rudy" Ruettiger was accepted to the University of Notre Dame in the fall of 1974 after completing two years at Holy Cross Junior College and four failed attempts at acceptance. Through sheer tenacity, he made the practice squad for the Irish, and on November 8, 1975, Coach Dan Devine put Rudy in the game against Georgia Tech. Historically, in order to officially be documented as a member of the roster, a player must record at least one play in a game. Rudy played three plays near the end of that game and, consequently, achieved his dream. He is one of only two players in Notre Dame history to be carried off of the field of play on his team's shoulders.

Perhaps even more noteworthy is the fact that Daniel Ruettiger also graduated from the University of Notre Dame in 1976. Interestingly, in spite of being the third of 14 children, Rudy was the first to graduate from college. And every Ruettiger boy after him went on to graduate.

By chasing his dream, Rudy not only accomplished it but also changed the lives of a legacy of men after him. He was truly the pivot point in his family between a life in the foundry and a life as a college graduate. And if Rudy did it, so can you.

Activation Questions

- *Have I ever had a dream? What was it?*

- *How did my immediate family respond to my dream?*

- *Looking back at the generations of men who came before me in me family, are they similar to each other (work, education, location, etc.)?*

- *Describe what it means to be a man in my family line.*

- *Does Rudy's dad sound familiar? If yes, how? If not, read on!*

13.

BOB, I NEED YOU TO ENGAGE
(The Absentee Dad at Home)

Y ears ago, I had a conversation with my son, Jordan, which had been a long time coming. I could detect some road-blocks in our relationship, and we were just having a casual discussion about life. If you are anything like I am, there are certain trigger mechanisms that can open the floodgate of latent anger or hurt, and I just happened to hit one of my son's during our time together. During the conversation, I learned some immutable facts about my relationship to Jordan, or at least how he perceived us. First, there were two video games he would never play again, although I can't offhand recall the names. Why? Because these were the two games he was playing when he learned that his mother and I were separating.

The second part of our collective past was that Jordan's memory of me (while a very young boy) was that I was simply never home. I could hear the disdain in his voice when he said, "You bowled all the time and you were never home." Truth be told, I only bowled on Tuesday nights from 9 p.m. until around 11:30 in a competition league, but to Jordan that was as good as "never home." In his defense, I did work a lot as well because I was tapped with the daunting title of "provider" and I was deeply engrossed in a failing business that had hired me to manage a drowning branch office. It ate up some hours, to say the least.

Add to that the simple fact that, at the time, life wasn't working out the way I had envisioned it when I was in my early twenties. I was stuck in a job I essentially hated with everything in me; was in a daily rut where I did precisely the same thing every day with no real forward progress; and, while I was the dad of two great kids, I was miserably unhappy in my marriage. My whole life was like a really bad chick flick, and I was the lead character, just hoping to find a way out. Maybe this sounds familiar to some of you.

While I do my best to keep the testosterone level of the movie clips I use during the live *Rough Cut Men* event as high as humanly possible, I have been known to occasionally throw in a cartoon. No, not Bugs Bunny or Fred Flintstone, but rather the digital characters created by none other than Disney/Pixar. Pixar has always been on the cutting edge of computer-generated cinema, and *The Incredibles* is still, without a doubt, one of my all-time favorites. If you have teens or 'tweens, my guess is you have watched this movie, and you may even be a closet fan. Case in point, I have a Mr. Incredible Christmas ornament I ritualistically put on our tree every year. One of our kids has, for years, been operating under the delusion that I am, in reality, Mr. Incredible. Who am I to shatter his dream?

While the overarching theme of *The Incredibles* is one of superheroes, there is a sharp undercurrent of a dysfunctional family. And the sad fact is it all revolves around the father figure, Mr. Incredible. The storyline of the movie is pretty simple, actually, probably due to the age range of the intended viewers. Mr. Incredible is a superhero, gifted with superhuman strength. He marries Elastigirl, who has the ability to stretch to astronomical proportions much like Mr. Fantastic from *The Fantastic Four*. After a string of unfortunate accidents and lawsuits involving a wide array of superheroes, the world ultimately determines that the "supers", as they are referred to by the media, are no longer needed or welcomed. So, one by one, the entire battery of the world's superheroes is placed in a superhero relocation program. Each one is given a new identity, home, and career as the population is purged of superheroes. Needless to say, Mr. Incredible and Elastigirl both fall prey to relocation and become an insurance claims adjuster and housewife, respectively. They become simply Bob and Helen Parr.

The Parrs are also blessed with three children, all possessing their own superhero skillset. Violet, their borderline "emo" teenage daughter, can turn invisible and create force fields. Consumed by a boy named Tony Rydinger, she perpetually has a dark cloud over her head and never speaks at a volume louder than a mumble. Dash is their elementary school-aged boy who can run at superhuman speeds, so fast that he is even undetectable on videotape. Their infant son, Jack Jack, doesn't display any superhuman abilities during the film, but if you happen to own the DVD and have watched the "Special Features" section, you quickly discover that Jack Jack can spontaneously combust and also become a big ball of lead. For some reason, I would love to have Jack Jack's talents, especially when standing in long bathroom lines at the baseball stadium. One quick ignition, WHOOF, and everybody's running, leaving all the stalls wide open. Admit it… that would be cool. However, due to the relocation, none of the kids are able to display their unique talents to anyone but their immediate family.

There is a dinner scene in the movie that exemplifies the dysfunction I alluded to earlier. Bob has just returned from yet another mundane day at the office and has somehow inadvertently destroyed the family car in the driveway. Like a trooper, Helen Parr attempts to spark up some conversation with the family by mentioning Dash had been sent to the office.

"Dash got sent to the office today," she informs Bob.

"Good, good," a completely disengaged Bob says, feigning interest.

"No, Bob, that's bad," Helen retorts. Apparently, Dash had put a tack on the teacher's chair during class, but he wasn't convicted of said crime due to the fact that even the videotape of the classroom showed no movement. After not only being rebuked by Helen for encouraging Dash to play pranks on the teacher but also cutting clean through a ceramic plate while assisting Dash with his steak knife, Bob dejectedly retreats into the kitchen.

What ensues is textbook banter between two kids, as Dash teases Violet incessantly about her love for Tony Rydinger, until an all-out yelling match results. Helen appeals to Bob, who is still in the kitchen.

"Kids, don't yell at the table... BOB!"

All that we hear from the other room is a flat monotone: "Kids, listen to your mother." He's no help to Helen.

Finally, an epic superhero confrontation breaks out between the two kids. Dash runs around the table at lightning speed, only to crash headlong into a forcefield thrown in his path by his sister. As Helen grabs one kid with one elastic arm and the other with another arm, she attempts to stop the melee. Dash and Violet refuse to stop the fight, darting under the table to resume the battle and stretching their mother's arms beyond their limits in the process.

Even with the clamor in the dining room, Bob settles into the kitchen to read the paper. As he notes an article about one of his former super-colleagues disappearance, Helen shouts, "Bob, it's time to engage! I need you to... INTERVENE!"

Bob's "intervention" involves hoisting the dining room table up in the air with both children and his bride still attached to it. If it wasn't for Frozone, yet another relocated "super", knocking on the Parr's front door, I can only imagine where that table was headed. Likely either through the wall or out the window!

This dinner scene can be eerily familiar to a lot guys, including me. Just as my son's recollection of who I was is pretty pathetic, my personal recollection of my dad isn't a lot better. Out of respect for my dad, let me first say my perception may not be the reality, but it is all that my mind shakes out about growing up with my folks. Since there is a very pronounced gap in my memory, I regress back to being around eight or nine years old most of the time.

As with a lot of kids growing up in the late 1960s and early 1970s, my father worked all day and my mother stayed home. I often refer to this time period in parenting as the "just you wait 'til your father gets home" era. Dad struck fear into my heart, especially as the disciplinarian. If I messed with my mother, my dad always showed up at precisely 6:30 p.m. to set me straight. But on most evenings during the early part of my life, when I wasn't destined for a swat on the butt, my dad had a ritual. He would check the mail, say "hello," and then sit down to watch Walter Cronkite on the CBS Evening News. And I usually just waited until those famous closing words, "And that's the way it is," followed by the much anticipated "I'm Walter Cronkite. Good night." It was then, and only then, that I felt I had his full attention.

I guess you could say I wrote another "story" in my life at this point. Not only did I never do anything right, but I was also not worth paying attention to. That's chapter two of my bad "story"—"everyone ignores me." Suffice it to say, this story has some pretty devastating subchapters.

Often, kids who don't get enough attention from Dad look for it elsewhere. In my case, I was the guy who always wanted to be the center of attention. I strived to be the life of the party and did my absolute best to be the loudest, most offensive guy I could be. After all, even negative attention was better than no attention at all, right? Young men who have this story tend to make some pretty bad judgment calls when it comes to who they hang out with and what they do with their free time. Young women, on the other hand, respond in a different way when they have the "ignore me" story. These girls are the ones who disregard the statement "modest is hottest." They wear clothes that are designed to draw attention to themselves and act in the same manner. And they get a lot of attention, mostly from the wolves that prey on young women who suffer from an uninvolved dad.

Since the beginning of the new millennium, some startling statistics have emerged with regard to children and absentee fathers. In 2006, while I was presenting the "Great Dads" fathering workshop, I learned that, of the 72 million kids in America under the age of 15, 24 million (that's a third) of these children go to bed without their biological father at home. Like many men in the church, I am a contributor to this statistic with both my own children and my stepkids. Perhaps even more crushing is that additional fact that, of those same 72 million children, 12 million kids have a father at home that is spiritually, physically, and even emotionally disengaged. Just like Mr. Incredible.

This would be an excellent time to step back and offer a couple of foolproof tips to avoid the inevitable disaster that can potentially develop through at-home father absence. I realize that in today's economy, everyone is working hard to barely survive, if they are working at all. The days of dad at work/mom at home have been trumped by the need to have two working parents just to make ends meet. But this is really about the quality of the time, not the quantity. So here are some do-it-yourself behavior modification tips that require little to no real effort. They say 21 days forms a habit, so take the next three weeks and give this **8-Step Plan** a shot:

1. When you pull into the garage, leave your laptop in the car. You can always rescue it later.

2. When you walk in the door, skip the mail. It isn't going anywhere.

3. First, greet your wife. Ask her about her day and then listen to her—without trying to fix anything. This models, to your children, just where your wife fits on your priority list.

4. Second, say "hello" to your kids. Ask them about their day. And listen.

5. In my case, the act of listening involves eye contact. Joni will stop mid-sentence if I am not looking into her eyes when she is speaking to me. Even if I can recite everything she has just said verbatim, it doesn't fly. So learn

how your wife feels heard and do it. If you don't know, ask her. And make eye contact when she tells you, if you know what's good for you.

6. If you have teenage daughters, tell them how beautiful they are. I have two teenage daughters, and I can assure you they rarely feel pretty. Words are free. So are hugs, so give your girls lots of attention. It's a hard thing to hear, men, but if you aren't loving on your daughter, someone else will be. Remember what being a teenage boy was like?

7. Remember that both your wife and your children do not need a quick fix or to hear "well, what I would have done is…" Look them in the face and listen to their words. You are only released to give an opinion when it is asked of you. Take it from the ultimate "fixer."

8. Have dinner together at the table any time you get the chance. Now I know what it's like to have church choir rehearsals, karate, and kids with jobs, but make the effort. It's worth it. Oh, and no texting at the table. That includes you, dude.

You are now hereby officially released to get your laptop and sift through the mail.

So what about Mr. Incredible? What is the deal with this superhero-turned-insurance guy who appears to have completely checked out of his family? Unlike Rudy's dad, who watched his own father jump ship, Mr. Incredible is quite different. This guy was created to be a superhero, complete with superhuman strength and a spandex outfit to go with it. But, due to circumstances beyond his control, he is pushing a pencil behind a desk. He has a burning passion to save people but isn't living out that passion. In fact, there is a scene where his wife discovers "rubble" on his shirt after Mr. Incredible sneaks out to save people from a burning building. He's miserable, to put it mildly, and the people who appear to suffer the most are his wife and his children.

If you have ever seen *The Incredibles* in its entirety, you discover that the superhero drought is a short-lived season. And Mr. Incredible, this time with the aid of his entire family, again saves the world from yet another master villain.

Maybe life hasn't worked out like you planned. Perhaps even over the past few years the economic downturn has affected you. Through no fault of your own, life just got ugly fast. Just the other day, a man who used to write seven-figure mortgages for a large residential lender handed me my food through a drive-thru window. It's humbling and sometimes even devastating to be knocked down like that. But take heart, brother.

Although it may not seem so right now, I can assure you this season will come to an end, as after every winter there is always a spring. You will get through this storm, but don't allow it to impact how you interact with your wife and your children. They are going to perpetuate your legacy, like it or not, so don't wreck it by feeling sorry for yourself. You have been called as the spiritual leader of your home, so shirking that responsibility is never an option. Jobs come and go, and money does, too, but you are first and foremost the steward of your marriage and your children. It's the highest calling bestowed on a man, so don't squander the time that you have buried in lament or regret.

Going back a generation, if you happen to be one of the men who grew up with a dad who was physically in the house but emotionally elsewhere, remember you can do it better than the other guy. Take a minute to reflect on how your father was, and then consider there may have been some mitigating circumstances that caused him to check out. Rest assured that it wasn't you, acknowledge that fact, and keep moving forward. It wasn't you; it was him.

Conversely, if you are one of the millions of men whose fathers were never in the picture in the first place, remember what Jesus told us about earthly fathers versus the love of our Father in heaven:

> *"Which of you, if his son asks for bread, will give him a stone? Or if he asks for a fish, will give him a snake? If you, then, though you are evil, know how to give good gifts to your children, how much more will your Father in heaven give good gifts to those who ask him."*   Matthew 7:9-11

The One who is love loves you more than you can fathom. And He also loves you more than any earthly father ever could. And that's truly all we need.

Activation Questions

- *Was my dad like Bob Parr (was he there but not really)?*

- *Has life worked out like I planned? What happened?*

- *Do I have balance between work and home? What needs to change?*

- *Can I commit to trying the 8-Step Plan for the next three weeks?*

14

MY PERSONAL JOURNEY WITH DAD
(God's Sovereignty Over a Bad Story)

I n light of Mr. Incredible, I thought I would share what God did in my relationship with my own father. There won't be any questions at the end of this chapter, but the Holy Spirit may just spark something deep within you that will spur you into action. In fact, literally every time that I share this story at a live *Rough Cut Men* event, some men are brought to tears because of a bad story that mowed over a father/son relationship. Don't breeze past this chapter, because God is still on the throne and He does remarkable things with His conviction and our obedience.

Recently, as I began to investigate my own "story," it became clear to me that perhaps I wasn't seeing things accurately. In fact, I had fabricated such a huge lie in my life regarding my own father that it literally impacted every part of my life. In light of the foregoing Father Wound chapters, I feel certain my personal story will somehow help another man get past not only a terrible "story" but also may help reconcile a once-damaged relationship between a father and a son.

Over the past near decade, I have spent an inordinate amount of time speaking to men, either in large groups or one-on-one. Men who are crushed by life, struggling with identity, and even battling major relationship issues. It's almost an epidemic these days, and for years now, I have been speaking about the issue at a gut level, citing some major "wounding" in my life.

Just so you know, I had spoken to my father exactly two times in the past four years, and not one of those conversations was longer than about 90 seconds. I even stopped calling on holidays just to avoid the rejection. I have lived much of my adult life thinking I was a monumental disappointment to my dad. It seemed that nothing I did was good enough, so I consequently developed a huge case of bitterness. And I have met a lot of guys just like me along the way.

At the beginning of 2012, God began to deal with me on almost every facet of my walk with Him. As I mentioned earlier, first it was tithing (or not tithing, actually). Then it was my quiet time (or complete lack of it). Then my prayer life. Every discipline was an epic fail, and near the beginning of 2012, I purposed myself to address each one in order to stand blameless before man and my God. And honestly, I was feeling pretty holy if not downright self-righteous at that time. Enter the big detonation in my life: God confronted me with unforgiveness, specifically directed toward my mother and father, and He compelled me to deal with it head on.

You see, I had also only spoken to my mother about six times in the past four years. Every call was received with a flat, unfeeling monotone, so I quickly abandoned calling her as well. So when God convicted me about "forgiving" my folks, I figured Mom would be an easier call than my former Navy EOD-turned-attorney Dad. Keep in mind that my father is an intensely personal man, so I am going to avoid going into great detail about what went down between us. But also keep in mind that even the mere re-telling of this story brings tears to my once blinded eyeballs.

The first call to my mother was pretty cordial, not to mention an inch deep and a mile wide. No depth. It confirmed in my heart that I was unwelcome and basically unwanted.

The following week, after God again hammered on me a little, I called her again. After the surprise in her voice wore off, God really opened up a nice talk. I told her what God was doing in my heart and then mentioned I really needed to speak to Dad. Her reply was simply, "I don't think that would be a good idea." WHAM! The punch in the gut that I expected. He really does hates me.

Being a sales guy in the past, I attempted to feel out the objection. She proceeded to tell me that, on October 9, 1987 (yep, women never forget), I had done irreversible damage to my father. During that time in my early adult years, I got hooked up with the wrong crowd and got into quite a bit of trouble. Let's just say there's a lot of truth to the Scripture "Bad company corrupts good character" (1 Cor. 15:33). As it turns out, my father spent several years trying to keep me out of trouble in more ways than one. She replayed all I had done, much of which God had graciously erased from my memory. She finished by saying that I never said "thank you" and I just stopped calling him. In fact, she said my dad, whose father, you'll recall, abandoned him when he was very young, once said, "Not many men know what it's like to be abandoned by their father and abandoned by their son." And while my mother wanted me to learn a tough lesson in 1987, my dad refused to quit on me. He, in fact, singlehandedly saved my future.

At that moment, God broke my heart for my 76-year-old earthly father. By this time, I was sitting in my garage in my car, and my wife kept checking on me. I sobbed, nearly uncontrollably, on the phone, and Mom told me it would all be okay. I repented to her and thought of sending him a letter. Then I determined I would fly across the country to see him, which I actually did mere weeks later on March 25, 2012.

Why do I share this with you? For years, I played the victim. I was a self-righteous, ungrateful, entitled punk kid. For 25 years, I harbored deep unforgiveness toward my parents when I should have been the one seeking it. Instead of saying "thank you" to my dad, I said, "Forget you."

Guys, evaluate your animosity. Allow God to search your heart. Maybe we're the ones who are wrong. Perhaps it's time to address it in your life, too? I knew it was time to set it straight with my father. So I did. Read on...

Over the course of 2011, I logged nearly 90,000 miles in the air. I had traveled around the country and hadn't as much as been late for a flight. This flight was perhaps the most intimidating one I had ever planned on taking. As I mentioned, March 25, 2012, marked the day I was to travel from Florida to Oregon to seek my father's forgiveness for 25 years of latent devastation I had caused to our relationship.

After preaching on that Sunday morning, I literally went from the pulpit to my already packed car for an hour drive to the airport. Of all days, this flight had a mechanical issue that put us more than 90 minutes behind schedule. When we finally landed in Atlanta, I had precisely 18 minutes to catch my connection. And, of course, it was five terminals away. I ran the whole way,

OJ style, only to find my plane pushed back and waiting to taxi. And it was the last flight to the west coast!

My plan had been to arrive in Oregon at 9:30 p.m., streak to my folks' house, and talk to my dad. Plan smashed. The airline put me up in a hotel, where I was given an additional 18 hours to pray about exactly what to say. In hindsight, it was a blessing, as I arrived the next day at noon feeling refreshed and much more awake than I likely would have been.

Mom answered the door and hugged my guts out. She said the traditional Mom-ism: "Let me look at you." It was an amazing homecoming, albeit for a brief few hours, since my father was still at work. As I pointed out earlier, since I am a child from the "just you wait 'til your father gets home" era, panic struck me as I heard the garage door going up. Then I heard his feet coming up the stairs, not nearly as fleet of foot as I remembered, as he was now over 75 years old.

"Hello, David," he said, reluctantly extending a hand and shunning my hug attempt. I guess I had a Southern Bell phone commercial reunion in mind, but instead I got nearly nothing. I had hoped for the best but planned for the worst, and I received pretty much what I had planned for. Simple pleasantries were exchanged, and I felt my cue to state the purpose of my visit. Through tears, I told him every word I had rehearsed in my mind. I told him I wanted nothing from him, but I wanted to apologize and cited specifics. Mom was moved to tears; Dad was summarily unfazed. I repented and asked for his forgiveness and then fell silent.

After what seemed like hours, my dad said, "Son, years ago you called me a [expletive deleted] after everything I did for you. I don't care who calls me that. That one is impossible to forgive."

And the hits kept on comin'. I had asked God to use me as light, and I was on a mission to be just that. I acknowledged his answer and recommitted to wanting a relationship with him whenever he was ready. As I got up to leave, I said, "This is why I flew here, and I have said what I came to say. I love you."

Then Mom threw an NBA pick on me as I tried to leave. "Let's have dinner," she said. My dad stared at me and said, "You said you've changed since then. What's different?" My only response was, "I am." It didn't dawn on me until later that "I Am" is God's name! And I believe God cracked just a little bit of Dad's heart toward me just then.

We did have dinner that night, and I caught them up on everything. Mom said, "Keep talking and keep asking questions." I had a hotel reserved, but my parents invited me to stay in a somewhat awkward situation, which I did (in my old room, even).

You know, each day got a little better. As I was preparing to leave for the return trip home, I hugged my dad and told him I loved him. I also asked his forgiveness again. This time he said, "I am really going to try. That's the best I can do right now." When I called him from home to again thank him for everything, he stated, "You know, son, I think this is all going to be just fine."

A word of counsel: while God forgives immediately, people take a while. Expecting 25 years of damage to evaporate overnight would have been ridiculous on my part. As we embark on missions of reconciliation, we must manage our expectations. And fuel them all with prayer. I had an army of people behind me who prayed well in advance of this trip. And God did exceedingly, abundantly beyond what I had imagined.

God gave me my dad back. And in his eyes, maybe, just maybe, who I am has shifted from a relational failure to a man of character who is leaving a legacy behind that will be worth talking about. My prayer is that he is talking well of me now. Don't wait to reconcile. Our very legacy depends on it.

Let's get back to our fathers in film and spend some time looking at the power of words.

15.

YOU KNOW WHAT YOU ARE? NOTHING!
(Words Hurt)

Have you ever sent an e-mail you wish you could unsend? You know the one I mean, right? You're seething mad at someone, you vent it all into your outbox, and then you just cavalierly launch it at them. My mother always said (not to sound like Forrest Gump), "You can't unring a bell." I'm always fascinated by those live courtroom shows where the prosecuting attorney is hammering away on the defendant and finally crosses the line. The defense attorney jumps up and says, "I object!" The judge agrees and sustains the objection. This is the part that kills me. The judge then turns to the jury and simply states, "The jury will disregard what they just heard." Are you kidding me with that? I don't know about you, but once I hear something, it will influence my decision whether it gets stricken from the record or not. What we hear affects how we think. Period.

What I'm really trying to say is hurtful words have a very long shelf life, and they can cause unintentional catastrophic damage. And, quite often, this damage resonates in the mind of the hearer or the reader for years, or decades, or even a lifetime.

I remember attending my first fathering seminar, where they continually reminded us that our kids need unconditional affirmation. "Go home and tell your kids how proud you are of them," the speaker challenged us. "They don't have to earn it. Just tell them you're proud of them!" Fired up to make a lifelong impact on my son, I hurried home to test out my new edification skills. He was probably only eight or nine years old at the time, and I scampered up the stairs to tell him the good news.

"Jordan," I said.

He looked up from whatever handheld video game console was popular at the time to reply, "Yeah, Dad?"

"Son, I just want you to know how proud I am of you," I beamed. As I sat there, waiting to receive my father of the year award, Jordan just stared blankly at me. "He's processing this awesome sentiment," I thought, mentally patting myself on the back.

Then, without an expression, he replied, "Why? I screw up all the time."

I knew, at that moment, I had failed as a father in more ways than I thought.

According to a research study at the University of Iowa, the average two-year-old child hears 432 negative statements per day but only 32 positive statements each day. And by the time your kid is in high school, he or she will hear an average of 15 negative comments to every one positive. Bottom line, gentlemen, is it begins and ends with us.

So what about the guy who, while growing up, heard words that cut him to the very core of his soul? Some men have heard statements that have literally created a lifelong nightmare for them, affecting marriages, careers, and interpersonal relationships as well. These damaging words can ultimately lead to addictive behaviors, chronic depression, and—in some cases—even suicide. The life of country singer Johnny Cash, as reflected in the Oscar winning movie *Walk the Line*, illustrates exactly the kind of words to which I'm referring.

Having five kids, we watch a lot of movies on DVD at my house. It's the only way we can afford it any more, as it typically costs about $50 just to feed a family of seven at McDonald's. Whenever I pick the movie, something needs to fly, blow up, or shoot something. And, if your house is anything like mine, it's our wives who bring the culture in and mitigate the testosterone levels whenever possible. Now my wife is not a fan of the classic "chick flicks" in the slightest, but she does like Oscar winners. I often joke with men that our wives pick out DVDs based strictly on the cumulative number of Oscar trophies on the box. And if you aren't careful, you'll spend the evening watching movies like *The Pianist, The English Patient,* or *Out of Africa.* Don't get me wrong; those are great films recognized for their cine-matic achievements. But there isn't a rocket-propelled grenade or hostage crisis in any of them. By and large, Oscar winners are usually pretty tame, with the obvious exceptions being *Saving Private Ryan* and *The Shawshank Redemption.* Shoot, even *Titanic* is epic, provided you cut out the whole "Jack Dawson meets Rose DeWitt Bukater" love thing.

That being said, when my wife suggested we watch *Walk the Line* on a recent date night (obviously we don't watch movies like *Walk the Line* or *Saving Private Ryan* with kids in the room), I felt the sudden need to go fix the flapper in the toilet or some-thing. "But it was nominated for five Academy Awards and I heard it was good," Joni informed me, as if it would make it any less painful to watch. Add to this the fact that the film is a pseudo-biographical account of the life of a country singer, and I don't even like country music. Having spent nearly two decades in the Pacific Northwest at the height of the grunge music revolution, I would have been more willing to entertain the idea if the movie was about Pearl Jam or Alice in Chains. So while the mere thought of watching an Academy Award-winning film about a country star was almost too much to bear, I fired up the DVD player and took one for the team. And *Walk the Line* became one of my all-time favorite movies.

Much to my surprise, *Walk the Line* was an eye-opener for me in more ways than one. First, I had no idea Johnny Cash rolled with the likes of Elvis Presley, Jerry Lee Lewis, and Waylon Jennings. He was, by all definitions, a rock star in his era. And he lived his young life as such, as he was wildly addicted to pills and alcohol for years. Secondly, I learned the words of a father can literally ruin a young man for the balance of his life. And this movie illustrates both perfectly.

Blending two film sequences from separate times in Johnny's life reflects just how devastating a father's words can be. Near the beginning of the film, Johnny's older brother Jack is killed in an accident by a malfunctioning table saw while cutting wood. Now it's no secret that Jack is their dad's favorite, and Mr. Cash makes it known often. Little Johnny, or "JR" as he's called, has gotten tired of waiting on his brother to finish the wood and is fishing under a bridge at the time of the accident. No one really knows exactly where Mr. Cash is.

While Jack, bloodied by the saw blade, is close to dying at home, Mr. Cash returns home with Johnny and literally drags him by the arm into the room where Jack is lying. In spite of the tears and JR's pleading to the doctor to "do something," Jack succumbs to his injuries. Johnny Cash was only 12 years old when his 15-year-old brother died.

After Jack's funeral, the scene again returns to the Cash family's small Arkansas home. Since it's only 1944, there is nothing more than a console radio playing music with Johnny sitting in front of it. Johnny's passion, at 12 and even right up until his death many decades later, is always music.

Angry and stumbling, Mr. Cash crashes through the front door, looking through empty cans in the kitchen. In a fit of quiet rage, Mr. Cash approaches Johnny and simply says, "You know what that is? *[He's referring to the music on the radio at this point]* Nothing. And that's what you are!" As little JR runs headlong into the bedroom to get away from his father, Mr. Cash erupts into a yelling tirade. "The devil did this! He took the wrong son!" he screams. Is it any wonder Johnny Cash ends up an emotional and physical trainwreck within a few years?

Moving forward in time roughly 15 years or so, Johnny Cash is now in his mid-twenties, is a world-renowned country music singer, and has already ruined one marriage while living almost every waking minute either drunk or whacked out on pills. The scene fades in with Johnny standing on the deck of his newly acquired lake house in Nashville. It's Thanksgiving, and his parents are visiting. His love interest, June Carter, is also arriving with her parents, while the tension between Johnny and his father continues toward a rolling boil.

In fact, it becomes clear Mr. Cash is dead set on verbally assaulting his now-famous son whenever possible. Even as an adult, Johnny's dad accuses him of not taking care of an expensive tractor; and when June and her family arrive for dinner, Mr. Cash states, "We were going to make dinner for ya'll, but Johnny here doesn't have a pot or a pan." You can just hear the unspoken "idiot" being used as a punctuation mark.

Johnny's addiction is no secret either, and he is completely inebriated throughout dinner, often nodding into a stupor. Finally, Johnny decides to say something at the table: "I'm really glad you all could be here today, Thanksgiving and all. Glad you came. Not everybody's here, are they, Daddy? Jack's not here, is he? I was 12 years old, you got Jack's bloody clothes, and you says to me, 'Where you been?' Remember what you said to me? You says, 'Where you been?'"

Mr. Cash responds simply, "Well, where were you?"

And Johnny fires back, "Where were YOU?"

It's amazing to me just how long hurtful words or actions can impact us as men. For nearly 15 years, Johnny Cash was living the life of someone who was "nothing." His father had clarified Johnny's position in the family by yelling that the devil had somehow taken the popular, athletic Jack instead of the meek, musical Johnny. And Johnny Cash did an incredible job of living up to his father's expectations.

No matter what Johnny Cash did, he would likely never be able to please his father. At the time of the Thanksgiving table meltdown, Johnny was an award-winning country musician, complete with gold records and hundreds of thousands of fans around the world. He was doing his absolute best to put a bandage on the devastating verbal wounding he received from his dad by both numbing the pain with drugs and alcohol and trying to achieve whatever he could musically in an attempt to please Mr. Cash. And we see, at Thanksgiving, that there's no pleasing his dad.

I'm happy to say that Johnny hits the wall, gets clean from his reliance on drugs and alcohol, and does indeed end up having a decent relationship with his father. But the question still remains as to why Mr. Cash felt it necessary to be so brutal to his young son. After all, Johnny didn't kill Jack with the saw; he was just a 12-year-old boy.

In order to understand the catalyst behind Johnny Cash's father wound, we again have to take a good look at the dad. It's worth repeating that behind every father wound you will often find a wounded father. Jack was Mr. Cash's firstborn son and, consequently, a source of great pride for his dad. Little JR just sort of hung out behind the scenes, falling in love with music along the way, and perhaps disappointing his farmer father a bit because of it. Mr. Cash was a "man's man," so to speak. The overarching problem had nothing to do with music or favoritism but rather their father's battle with alcohol.

Do you remember Mr. Cash's search through the empty cans prior to verbally assaulting little Johnny by the radio? He was looking for beer money. Do you know where Mr. Cash was while Jack was falling into that saw blade? He was at a bar. So on Thanksgiving, when Johnny asked his dad, "Where were you?" that question had to cut Mr. Cash pretty deep.

Were you one of those guys like Johnny, with a father who called you "nothing"? Or maybe you grew up with an abusive, alcoholic father? I meet lots of men who are textbook "Johnnys." The one common thread that runs through these men is the constant question "what did I do to make my dad hate me so much?" or "what did I do to make my dad leave?" You need to know it wasn't you. It was him. And, above all else, as hard as it may seem, Jesus commands us to forgive him. It doesn't mean we will be Beaver Cleaver with a perfect life, but rather we need to be freed from the chains of anger and unforgiveness. I know it's easier said than done, but you will be liberated from both hurt and ownership of the outcome.

If you happen to be the dad who fired away relentlessly at your son, today is the day to reach out to him and say, "I'm sorry." Tell him about your past so he completely understands who you are as a man, not just as his father. Tell him about your own dad so your apology cuts through the wall that has been built. Every son needs a dad, and every dad needs a son. Maybe you've been holding on to the hurt for way too long, and it's time to set the record straight and get back to being father and son.

Most importantly, if you are neither the wounded son nor the bitter father, here is one way to make sure you don't say something you later wish you could "unsay." Before you speak, first pray it's the right thing to say and the right time to say it. And then measure your words before you say them with this three-step gauge:

1. Is what I am about to say TRUE?

2. Is what I am about to say KIND?

3. Is what I am about to NECESSARY?

These three questions are the litmus test for whether we should open our mouths in the first place. And I mean it has to pass *ALL THREE STEPS*, not just one or two. It must be true, meaning it isn't embellished or enhanced into inaccuracy just to make a point. It must be kind, meaning would Jesus say it? You don't have to decorate it in flowers before you say it, but there is no room for caustic words. Remember, they have a very long shelf life in our lives. And third, is it necessary? In other words, is what I am about to say going to mean anything in a few hours or am I just saying it to get in one final low blow? Remember, if it isn't true AND kind AND necessary, just walk away.

Think about the power of words in light of the Bible. In Genesis, when God was in the middle of creating everything, almost every verse begins with three words: "And God said." The entire world in which we live was created with words out of the mouth of a holy God. No other actions were needed. He simply spoke the world into existence.

In chapter one of the Gospel of John, it begins with the following: "In the beginning was the Word, and the Word was with God and the Word was God." Jesus is the Word. That's not a description of Jesus but an actual name for Jesus.

Do you remember the story of Jesus and the fig tree? The Lord was walking along with some of His disciples and told a fig tree it would never bear fruit again. A few days later, the disciples walked past that same tree only to find it completely dead and defoliated. They were amazed at the power of the words spoken by Jesus and subsequent destruction of a tree.

The Bible says the same power that raised Jesus from the dead lives in us, and we consequently have the same power when it comes to our words. One Proverb even goes as far as to say that words have the power to give life and to bring death. As men, we have the power to not only bless our kids but also curse them if we aren't careful.

Fathers, do not exasperate your children; instead, bring them up in the training and instruction of the Lord.

Ephesians 6:4

Imagine how much smoother Johnny Cash's life would have been had his father not called him "nothing" in an alcoholic fueled rage. While his father's emotional outburst had absolutely nothing to do with Johnny, it still impacted young Cash adversely for an extraordinarily long time. Some things are just better left unsaid.

Do not let any unwholesome talk come out of your mouths, but only what is helpful for building others up according to their needs, that it may benefit those who listen.

Ephesians 4:29

Activation Questions

- *Do I remember words my father said that may have hurt me? If yes, how long is a reasonable time to hang on to those words?*

- *Do I know men who had a father like Mr. Cash? How can I help them recover from that wounding as we travel together?*

- *Have I ever said anything to my kids that I wish I hadn't said? How would I do it differently, knowing words can last a lifetime?*

16.

TELL ME I'VE BEEN A GOOD MAN
(Living a Life Worth Repeating)

D eep within the heart of every man is the desire to finish
well. Regardless of how we may have started, one of our
greatest visions is to leave a story behind that will be retold with
pride. And, on top of that, almost every guy wants to do it better
than the other guy—the man or men who have come before us.
If we are able to overcome the "story" we have believed for so
long, we liberate ourselves not only from unforgiveness but also
from the legacy of the men before us who may have not done it
quite right. Or maybe we've got to get past our own failures in
the past and create an entirely new legacy of what it means to be
a godly man in our lineage.

Saving Private Ryan is, at least in my opinion, perhaps the
best World War II movie ever filmed. After interviewing dozens
of men who were actually "boots on the ground" at Omaha
Beach on June 6, 1944 (aka, D-Day), director Steven Spielberg
was able to visually illustrate the statement "war is hell." The initial war scene in the film depicts Germans in overhead positions
firing high caliber machine guns directly into the dropped gates
of the Allied transports, beaches peppered with both landmines
and bodies, and water turned red from the blood of the first
soldiers to hit the beach. It's graphic, it's awful, and the viewer
fully understands that literally thousands of kids never made it
to June 7, 1944.

Up until *Saving Private Ryan*, we had movies like 1962's *The Longest Day*, another Academy Award-winning film, starring the heroes of that cinematic era—John Wayne, Henry Fonda, and Robert Mitchum. And for many decades, boys all over the world owned little green plastic army helmets and wanted to be soldiers more than anything. I recall a scene where several stars of *The Longest Day* are standing on the beach, smoking cigarettes, and having a "water cooler" type discussion while bullets are flying all around them. While obviously much more graphic due to the advancements in cinematography, *Saving Private Ryan* shows us just how unlikely it is that a normal conversation would have occurred, and how equally unlikely it would have been to be casually smoking with artillery zinging past the heads of the officers in question.

Using a flashback format, *Saving Private Ryan* begins with an old man shuffling down a random sidewalk in the American Cemetery, located above that very same Omaha Beach in France. His extended family is in tow, and they are all dumbfounded as to where he is going or why. In fact, the general discussion between the old man's adult children appears to revolve around him being either old or crazy. Then the movie backs up to June 6, 1944.

Tom Hanks portrays Captain John Miller, who leads a company of men onto the beach at Normandy on D-Day. While he does lose several of his men during the attack, Miller succeeds in overtaking one of the Nazi overhead positions, thereby opening a door for the US forces to take the beach. Shortly after successful mission number one, Miller is asked by his commanding officer to take on a new assignment—one which has come down directly from the War Department. You see, there is a woman named Mrs. Ryan who has four sons involved in the war effort, and three of them have already been killed in action. In an effort to avoid sending poor Mrs. Ryan four telegrams instead of three, the War Department determines that the last remaining Ryan boy needs to come home. And Captain Miller is tasked with the responsibility of finding this young man, Private James Ryan (played by Matt Damon), who is somewhere in France.

Pulling together a ragtag group of seven soldiers, Miller sets off to locate the man he refers to as "a needle in the pile of needles." Unfortunately for the team, James Ryan's paratrooper division missed their landing zone by hundreds of miles, and the majority of the flashback is spent locating Ryan. After losing two men, Miller and his crew track Ryan down, but he refuses to go home. Instead, when told of his brothers' deaths and of the Army's desire to send him home, Ryan says, "Tell her that when you found me, I was here and I was with the only brothers that I have left." James Ryan wasn't about to leave his platoon, nor was he going to stand idly by while more men died.

The platoon ends up in Ramelle, where they decide to ambush a division of Nazis who happen to be accompanied by a battery of tanks and artillery. A plan is devised to destroy the only remaining bridge in Ramelle, thereby thwarting the German plans to push forward. During the subsequent engagement, even more of Miller's men die, leaving him with only two soldiers from the original platoon. US airplanes arrive just in time to negate the German advancement, but Miller is shot in the chest while attempting to detonate the explosives placed under the bridge.

Nearly dead, John Miller calls James Ryan to his side, grabs the young man by the shirt to pull him close, and offers some powerful words to the young Private "James," Miller says. "Earn this. Earn it." What Captain Miller is really saying, in a nutshell, is, "Don't forget that five, going on six, men died so you can go home and be with your mommy and grow old. Don't waste it." Given how much resentment the other soldiers have toward Ryan after searching the French countryside for him, these words are a powerful reminder to James Ryan that his legacy has carried a tremendous cost. The scene slowly fades back into present day, into the cemetery, where a now much older James Ryan stands at the foot of the headstone of Captain John Miller.

Remember when I said words have a long shelf life? James Ryan, no longer 20 years old, but now 80, replays the last words of John Miller to the grave: "Every day I think about what you said to me that day on the bridge. I tried to live my life the best that I could. I hope that was enough. I hope that, at least in your eyes, I've earned what all of you have done for me." James Ryan had not only remembered the words spoken by John Miller but purposed himself to live by them while remembering how many men gave their lives so he could live his. Then, from the crowd of family gathered behind Ryan, his wife walks up. The old man turns, looks his wife directly in the eyes, and nearly begs her, "Tell me I've led a good life. Tell me I'm a good man." Without the slightest hesitation, his wife confirms, "You are."

As I have watched this scene well over a thousand times, I note new things virtually every time. As the aforementioned scene closes, the camera begins to slowly pan forward, ultimately ending with nothing more than James Ryan's back facing the single cross-shaped tombstone of his former commanding officer. Very recently, as the words "earn this" echoed in my mind, I realized Jesus has never asked me to earn what He did for me on that cross. Jesus Christ took the nails in His hands and feet, bearing my past, present, and future sin on His shoulders, and died freely to liberate me from sin and to secure a spot for me in heaven for all eternity. It may have been a while since you have pared salvation down to the death on the cross, since we men like to overcomplicate everything. But the simple fact is this: Jesus died and rose three days later so that we can spend eternity with Him, and He finished the job simply because He loves us. Nothing more and nothing less. Now don't get me wrong, we should WANT to do everything we can to advance His kingdom. But Jesus never put a conditional on accepting His sacrifice for us… there is no "earn this."

Another interesting observation I made recently while watching this scene truly reveals the nature of men. As I have said before, we are a pretty tight-lipped bunch of dudes, allowing almost no one into our "inner circle," so to speak. We keep everyone outside the walls so we don't get hurt. Sometimes even our wives. As James Ryan is mulling over his life and the death of his friend many decades earlier, the first thing his wife says upon arriving next to him is, "Captain John H. Miller." At last, the great mystery of why this old man was walking through the cemetery is revealed and his wife now knows who James was searching for among the tombstones. What strikes me as odd is the way Mrs. Ryan says the name. She says "Captain John H. Miller" with sort of a "who the heck is this guy?" tone. Isn't the only reason there is a man standing in front of that headstone is because of the man lying under it? I mean, Ryan would have also died in France were it not for John Miller. So how is it that, after 50-plus years, James Ryan has never told his bride about the man who literally saved his future? As I work with men in the military, I realize that a lot of guys who've been "downrange" never talk about it. What is seen in the theater of battle is secret. Yes, men are tough nuts to crack. We don't talk to anyone.

You know, one day in the not so distant future, each of us will have to stand before our God in heaven and give a recount of our lives. Essentially, we get to watch an ESPN replay of sorts, depicting how well we did as kingdom guys. Every touchdown, every interception, every rumble, and every fumble. My prayer, not only selfishly for myself but also for every guy reading this, is we hear the words:

> *"Well done, good and faithful servant! You have been faithful with a few things; I will put you in charge of many things. Come and share your master's happiness!"*
>
> *Matthew 25:23*

And just like James Ryan, I want to be able to look not only my wife but also anyone I have encountered during my life right in the face and hear the words: "You are a good man." We all want to be able to stand before everyone we know and say something similar to what Samuel said as he was entering the closing minutes of his life:

> *"Here I stand. Testify against me in the presence of the Lord and his anointed. Whose ox have I taken? Whose donkey have I taken? Whom have I cheated? Whom have I oppressed? From whose hand have I accepted a bribe to make me shut my eyes? If I have done any of these, I will make it right."*
>
> *1 Samuel 12:3*

Perhaps the most exhilarating thing about being a part of the kingdom of God is the simple fact God allows us to mess up and to repent. No matter what we've done with our lives to date, we are still vertical and still breathing. That means it's not too late to change others' perceptions from "you know, I really don't know what to think about that guy" to "he's a good man."

And it doesn't matter how the other guys before us did it or how old we are today. No matter how we started this race, we can still hear "well done" on our last days, both from man (or woman) and from God.

Remember, the only thing we truly leave behind is what other people are saying about us. Let's leave a life behind that is worth repeating. Let's finish well!

Activation Questions

- *How much thought have I given to my legacy?*

- *If I asked "Am I a good man?" would my wife's answer be just like Mrs. Ryan's? How would my kids answer?*

- *If I am not happy with the answers I think I might get, what can I do to effect change today?*

17.

THE END OF THE WORLD
(The Last Impression)

Recently, I asked a roomful of 20-something recovering drug addicts one simple question: "Who was Joe Paterno"? Needless to say, I asked the question directly on the heels of Coach Paterno's death, mostly to confirm a suspicion I had about legacy. The first hand that went up was called upon, and his answer was simple enough: "He was that coach who did something to cover up what that other guy did to those kids. He's dead." He was, of course, referring to the 2012 Penn State University child abuse scandal revolving around assistant football coach Jerry Sandusky and head football coach Joe Paterno's alleged involvement in a massive cover-up of the numerous accusations. As a result of these accusations, Coach Paterno was fired and mere months later died of complications due to lung cancer. Penn State University was later hit with severe penalties from the NCAA, and Coach Paterno's statue was even removed from the front of the Nittany Lion stadium.

What shocked me the most about this young man's reply was the simple fact he knew nothing about Joe Paterno. "JoePa," as he was known among the football faithful, coached the Penn State Nittany Lions for 46 years, and up until the NCAA stripped him of wins that occurred during the time of the allegations, was the winningest coach in the history of NCAA Division I football. In the realm of college football, Joe Paterno was legendary. But in the eyes of the young man I met, he was nothing more than a dead guy who was involved in child abuse. To this young man, this was Joe Paterno's legacy.

Unless your name is plastered on the side of a new cancer wing at a hospital or you happen to be in a hall of fame somewhere, the whole concept of "legacy" can be boiled down to one concept: it's really nothing more than what other people are saying about us after we aren't around anymore. In fact, the only way the story of our life can continue is through the words of the people we leave behind. And in many cases, if you had a later-in-life conversion experience like I did, there are people out there who remember the older version of "us." Consequently, their review may not be too positive.

For however long the season a relationship may be, people remember us. And it's usually their last interaction with us that determines exactly what that legacy will be. Let's face it. We are all leaving a legacy behind, so it's up to us to determine what that legacy will be. What's even more compelling is the fact that our legacy sometimes varies depending on who you happen to interview. Because of this, I have arrived at the following statement that can be either encouraging or sobering based on who you happen to think about in this context. It simply says:

"Your last impression is your lasting impression"

In other words, the last time someone sees you is likely how they remember you. Period. To them, that last discussion or phone call encapsulates your legacy. I don't know about you, but that thought really bugs me, probably because I know I left a trail of devastation behind me before I met Jesus.

As a part of the ongoing mission of *Rough Cut Men*, I work with Teen Challenge Men's Centers all over the country. Their principal mission is truly Christ-centered drug rehabilitation, focusing on recovery from addiction and developing spiritual disciplines with their year-long residents. Basically, the men who are in the program are often there of their own volition, checking out of life for an entire year in order to get themselves right. Often, men graduate the Teen Challenge program and immediately enter seminary or become staff at one of the hundreds of centers worldwide.

While working with the Teen Challenge men, I hear some downright horrifying stuff about their histories. Guys who have upcoming court dates for armed robbery, assault with a deadly weapon, burglary, and even domestic violence. Addiction drives people to do some pretty insane things, and most of these men are no different. And as I speak to these guys, I call them out on those damaged relationships. After all, if the last impression was the lasting one, many of these men have left a legacy of crime and violence.

As the Lord changes the heart in the men at Teen Challenge, their desire to finish well becomes a key player. And a big part of finishing well is the legacy we leave after we break the yellow tape at life's finish line. These men, humbled and often completely broken, write letters and make calls to the people they have wronged. And many times they receive nothing in return. But they make the first move to change their legacy in the minds of everyone they have touched. We should follow their lead!

Have you ever seen the movie *Armageddon*? If you aren't a die hard (yeah, bad pun) Bruce Willis fan, then you may have overlooked this science fiction disaster film. The concept is pretty ridiculous actually, with a giant asteroid rocketing toward the earth. NASA has deemed this flying rock a "global killer," as the direct impact will invariably destroy the earth.

Devising a plan to blow the asteroid in half with a nuclear weapon, NASA solicits the advice of Harry Stamper (aka, Bruce Willis), a roughneck offshore oil well driller. When Stamper sees NASA's proposed drill and drill team, he offers to not only design a drill bit capable of chewing through the asteroid but also volunteers his entire drill team to assist in space. His team consists of convicted felons, gamblers, his daughter Grace (played by Liv Tyler), and his right hand man AJ (played by Ben Affleck). By the way, Harry spends much of the movie trying to kill AJ, as the young man has been after Stamper's daughter for a long time. There's no love lost between Harry and AJ.

The NASA plan involves sending up two space shuttles (the *Freedom* and the *Independence*) with two drills to ultimately land on the asteroid. There is a redundant system in place, in case one team doesn't make it. The first shuttle team to reach the 800-foot drill depth wins according to NASA, but their plans do not include the crash of one shuttle, the loss of several drill bits, and ultimately, the loss of an entire drill. Somehow surviving the crash of his shuttle, AJ arrives at the last minute with the only remaining drill and drill bit, and the team reaches the 800-foot depth just in time. Upon their lowering the nuclear weapon intended to destroy the asteroid into the hole, a problem with the remote detonator arises. The initial plan involved flying away from the asteroid prior to pushing the button, but now someone has to stay behind to set off the nuclear weapon. And being a Bruce Willis movie, who do you think stays behind to save the world? All I can say is: "Yippee-kai-yay."

After deciding to be "the guy," Harry Stamper makes a call from a video camera to his daughter, who is sitting in Houston at Mission Control awaiting the return of both her father and her fiancé, AJ. Here's the dialogue of that 30-second call:

Grace Stamper: *[talking to Harry on the monitor]* Daddy?

Harry Stamper: Hi Gracie. Hi honey. Grace, I know I promised you I was coming home...

Grace: I don't understand.

Harry: It looks like I'm going to have to break that promise.

Grace: I lied to you too, when I told you I didn't wanna be like you...because I am like you. And everything good that I have inside of me, I have from you. I love you so much, Daddy. And I'm so proud of you. I'm so scared. So scared.

Harry: I know it, baby. But there won't be anything to be scared of soon. Gracie, I want you to know that AJ saved us. He did. And I want you to tell Chick that I couldn't have done it without him. None of it. I want you to take care of AJ. I wish I could be there to walk you down the aisle but I'll...I'll look in on you from time to time, okay honey? I love you, Grace.

Grace: I love you too.

Harry: Gotta go now honey.

Grace: Daddy, no! *[Harry cuts the video feed]* No. No Dad, no!

Harry Stamper is given less than a minute to set the record straight with his only child right before his life is over. He actually does a pretty good job, too, as he apologizes to her, affirms her fiancé AJ, and even assures her everything is going to be okay. And Grace gets the chance to apologize for all of the nasty things she had said to her father during course of the film.

God is pretty clear on just how little we know about when we're going to live our last day:

Why, you do not even know what will happen tomorrow. What is your life? You are a mist that appears for a little while and then vanishes.

James 4:14

The bottom line is really simple, men. Since we have no guarantees we will even get up tomorrow, and since what other people are saying after we die is our legacy, then we should have a tremendous urgency to set the record straight with whomever we have mowed over in the past.

We should have zero tolerance for strained or broken relationships, and our legacy is in jeopardy if we don't begin the process of rebuilding now.

I know, I know! You're sitting there wondering why anyone, including God, would care about what one man did or didn't do. As if one man can make a difference, right? Check this out:

Have you ever heard of Easy Eddie? If you're like I was before I heard his story, that answer is probably a "no." What about Al Capone? Have you ever heard of Al Capone? He was the godfather of the modern day mafia godfathers. The founder of the modern day mob movement. In the 1920s, Capone was into everything from politics, to sanitation, to alcohol, to horse racing. And while Al Capone was a "white collar" criminal, he was also either directly or indirectly responsible for an awful lot of dead guys, including 1929's "Valentine's Day Massacre."

Unbelievably, Al Capone was rarely charged or convicted of any crime, partly due to the closed-mouth nature of the mob. At one point, he was charged with three murders but was released the next day due to a "lack of evidence." Ironically, what ultimately put Capone in jail wasn't a capital crime but rather just

23 counts of tax evasion. And the man who was largely responsible for Capone's uncanny ability to avoid convictions was Easy Eddie. Not because of his amazing marksmanship or corrupt talents but rather because Easy Eddie was, in fact, Al Capone's lawyer.

There are many recounts of the tales of Al Capone and almost as many about Easy Eddie, and I have been able to glean some consistent information about Capone's attorney. Eddie was apparently very good at the law game and was actually one of Capone's "hole cards." It's my understanding Capone protected Eddie, including physically building his lawyer a large house with a wall in Chicago. In other words, Capone really covered his asset. Now the story goes that the only thing in the world Eddie really loved was his son. And at some point, Easy Eddie likely decided he wanted to leave a different legacy behind for his son, so he turned state's evidence against Al Capone.

Very few men have ever turned on the mob and lived to tell about it. One of those men is Henry Hill, who you may remember from the movie *Goodfellas*, which is based on the Hill's life. Unfortunately, Easy Eddie is not one of the survivors of testifying against the mafia, as he was killed within a year of leaving Capone's organization. And so ends the life and legacy of Easy Eddie.

Fast forward to World War II. In 1942, while on a mission to bomb a series of enemy targets, the aircraft carrier USS Lexington had its position compromised by a Japanese spy plane. As a result, nine Japanese bombers were headed in the direction of the Lexington and six US Wildcat fighter planes launched off the deck to meet the Japanese head on. One of the Wildcats was piloted by Lt. Butch O'Hare from Chicago. In fact, you may have actually heard the name "O'Hare" when referencing the city of Chicago, as one of the international airports is named "O'Hare International." Yes, the airport is named after Butch, and here's why.

As O'Hare and his wingman were the first to dive into the oncoming Japanese bombers, it was clear the other US fighters in their sortie were not going to make it in time to engage the enemy before the Japanese released their payload directly onto the Lexington. What's even worse is that Butch's wingman had an issue with jammed machine guns. This left Lt. Butch O'Hare to repel the Japanese attack by himself. As the other US planes watched, O'Hare systematically shot down five of the nine bombers and ultimately ran out of ammunition in the process. Fortunately, the other US warbirds arrived in time to finish the job, and Butch was decorated with the Congressional Medal of Honor for saving his ship from certain destruction.

If you ever go to O'Hare International Airport in Chicago, you will find a statue of Lt. Cdr Butch O'Hare. You will also see his Medal of Honor as well as read the accolades of this amazing fighter pilot.

The one piece of information you likely won't see about Butch O'Hare? He was actually Easy Eddie's son. The minute a mob lawyer decided to do life a little differently, a war hero was born. So don't tell me one man can't change a legacy!

Changing the way people see us, and consequently our legacy in their eyes, takes intentional reconciliation. Most of the time with us men, these conversations intended to set things right take place when one party or the other is dying. And sometimes it never happens.

Think about the story I shared about flying across the country to see my dad. Over the years, we both ended up thinking the other guy wanted nothing to do with us. And the silence and anger just perpetuated it. What if I hadn't flown to Portland to see him? My guess is that, had I died with the situation unreconciled, his review of me would have been pretty bad. My legacy would have been one of profanity, anger, and abandonment. But what would he say about me now, especially in light of that trip to apologize? My prayer is that his perception of me now, my legacy in his eyes, would be one of humility and love. Or at least not as bad as I was, right?

To change our legacy in the eyes of those we have hurt requires we make the first move. If you wait around for them to call, it may never happen. And since we get to own 100% of our 50% of this relationship and we have been called to be reconcilers, guess what we have to do? We have to reach out to them and ask for forgiveness—or, in some cases, extend it to someone. Before you get all caught up in the validation of, "well, you don't know what they did to me" or "I can never forgive someone who did that," remember God has given us both a command and a conditional on forgiveness:

> *Be kind and compassionate to one another, forgiving each*
> *other, just as in Christ God forgave you.*
>
> *Ephesians 4:32*

We are commanded to forgive others as Christ forgave us. And He forgives us unconditionally, regardless of what we've done to Him. To make matters a little more pressing, check out the conditional found in the Lord's Prayer:

"...And forgive us our sins, as we have forgiven those who sin against us"

Matthew 6:12 (NLT)

Basically, by praying this prayer, we are giving God the green light to forgive us to the extent that we forgive other people. With that in mind, if we choose to hang on to unforgiveness, it's pretty crazy of us to think God will be doing much forgiving on our end. It's cause and effect, simply put. So if your legacy is being impacted by unforgiveness, it's high time to put it to bed and be the witness for Christ and let it go. Move on!

On the other hand, as with a lot of us, we leave a trail of destruction in our path when we chose to live a life separated from God.

Since I travel a lot, I have also unfortunately seen a few accidents on the freeways. I've even seen the carnage that results when a person decides to drive the wrong way on the interstate. Imagine for a minute that life is just like the freeway. In my case, for 25-plus years, I lived a life apart from the kingdom of God. I was not a nice guy, and I consequently destroyed a lot of relationships along the way. In essence, I was driving the wrong way down the freeway, smashing into every car (or person) I could. We're talking about driving 70 MPH directly into other people going 70 MPH.

We read in 1 John that God is quick to forgive, provided we repent.

If we confess our sins, he is faithful and just and will forgive us our sins and purify us from all unrighteousness

1 John 1:9

In other words, when we realize we are going the wrong direction, God forgives us and provides an immediate off-ramp that allows us to turn around and drive the right way. But here's the catch. God's forgiveness is immediate. People, not so much.

So as we are now pointed in the right direction thanks to God's grace, we stop crashing into oncoming traffic. However, we also get to see all of the carnage we've caused while we were going headlong into traffic. There are smashed up cars, fires, and wounded people lying on the pavement. While God forgives, I think we sometimes tend to forget just how much damage we caused in the lives of others, just as I had done with my dad. With him, I had convinced myself he was the problem, not me. I even cited Matthew 10 to validate I was right and he wasn't:

> *Do not suppose that I have come to bring peace to the earth. I did not come to bring peace, but a sword. For I have come to turn "a man against his father, a daughter against her mother, a daughter-in-law against her mother-in-law—a man's enemies will be the members of his own household."*
>
> *Matthew 10:34-36*

I had somehow deluded myself into thinking my relationship with God had somehow supernaturally caused the breakdown between my father and me. And, as you read, it was my mother who called me to account and showed me the error of my ways.

I believe God often sort of erases the memories of all of the bad stuff we did before we were saved, and He indeed may, but that certainly doesn't mean the other person has been so fortunate. So while we've moved on to greener pastures, our legacy of ill will continues in the minds of those we trampled over on the path to salvation. And our legacy suffers from it until we attack it like men of God.

There is a really funny scene in the Adam Sandler movie *Billy Madison* that really illustrates my point. Billy Madison is the adult son of a hotel tycoon played by Darren McGavin. There comes a point where Billy's dad decides to pass the hotel chain off to a successor, and the VP of the company is tapped with the privilege of becoming the new CEO. But Billy, a guy in his twenties who spends all day with two other buddies drinking and floating in the pool, protests that he is next in line. After a good laugh, Billy's father gives him one chance to take over the business.

In order to become the company president, Billy Madison must first go back to school, and not just to graduate, but to literally re-take every grade from first grade to twelfth grade. So for two weeks each, Billy is relegated back to school. Along the way, he makes some new friends and also has an epiphany of sorts when he reaches high school. As he endures high school and all of the bullying for being a rocker in an emo world, Billy suddenly remembers a boy by the name of Danny McGrath (played by Steve Buscemi). Billy had picked on Danny relentlessly, and he ultimately makes a decision to track him down to apologize for being so mean to him more than a decade earlier.

As Danny picks up the phone, Billy simply apologizes for the way he treated him. To his surprise, Danny doesn't remember anything about it and says it's no big deal. They exchange a few more pleasantries, and Billy hangs up, exonerated of the guilt he was feeling. Danny hadn't remembered anyway!

However, we discover something about the power of an apology as the camera returns to Danny McGrath's home. After hanging up the phone, Danny turns around to reveal a small sheet of paper on the wall behind him. The page is titled "People to Kill," and Billy Madison's name is on it. In one move, Danny strikes a line through Billy's name.

Don't ever underestimate the power of an apology. While we may have forgotten, the other person may still be hanging onto it.

By now, God has already placed on your heart a person or people who you need to reach out to and reclaim a positive legacy. And you may be tempted, just like I was, to call the easy person. After all, calling my mother was way less painful than calling my dad. But as the saying goes, "If you have to swallow a bunch of frogs, swallow the big one first." Take the most challenging person on your list, and get started.

There is a three-step plan to moving toward reconciliation:

1. Decide how you are going to contact them. If they are nearby, go see them. Avoid e-mail, as people can put whatever inflection they choose on your words and the message may get lost through the filter of anger. Letters aren't much better, as a person who thinks you are a jerk will likely make the letter sound like you are. The other option is a phone call, but know your script before you dial. Don't make it about you. Avoid words like "I need this." This is about humbling yourself and assuring them you are a new creation in Christ. Then shut up.

2. Share your plan with another man or two. Give them permission to check in to see how your progress is coming along. Tell them to ask until you follow through, and then

encourage them to continue to follow up with you as you rebuild what was shattered.

3. Pray before you embark on this mission. Get people praying for you for favor before you approach the person from whom you intend on seeking forgiveness. And manage your expectations. Don't expect a glorious reunion, and respond as Jesus would if you get return fire.

Proverbs 22:1 reads, **"A good name is more desirable than great riches, to be esteemed is better than silver or gold"**

We have to finish well, regardless of how we started. Our name is all we have. The words people are saying about us are often our only legacy.

Do you remember Samuel in the Bible from a few chapters back? He was responsible for finding both King Saul and King David for the Lord. He was a prophet who had a spotless reputation and frequently heard directly from God Himself. At the end of his life, he actually stood in front of the entire nation of Israel and confirmed he did it right. He asked each person in the crowd to call him out if there was anything in his life that wasn't above reproach. Basically, he asked, "Who have I wronged?" and assured them he would make it right before he went home to be with God. That's our mission, too.

It's worth repeating that we should have zero tolerance for broken relationships. Our legacy hinges on what others are saying. Our wives, our children, our parents, our siblings, and even our colleagues are going to be talking about us after we're gone. It's up to us to determine what they will be saying. And if there is someone out there who would give you a less than stellar report, change it.

Activation Questions

- *Who has God placed on my heart to reconcile with?*

- *How will I contact them?*

- *Have I shared this plan with my wingman to solicit his feedback and prayer?*

- *What will the impact be on my personal legacy as I strive to restore this particular broken relationship?*

18.

ONLY TAKE WHAT YOU NEED
(Dealing with Financial Suicide)

H ollywood has depicted some pretty amazing train crashes over the past few decades. The train crash scene at the beginning of *The Fugitive* is epic, as is the scene in Will Smith's *Hancock* where he jumps directly in front of a moving train to prevent it from smashing into a car stalled on the tracks. Subway crashes are just as numerous and can be seen in monumental derailments in the likes of Nicolas Cage's movie *Knowing*, Keanu Reeves' *Speed*, and—of course—Bruce Willis' *Die Hard with a Vengeance*

While all are markedly different with regard to location, theme, and actor, there is one very common concept illustrated universally in just about every Hollywood crash we see. The front car, or the engine, is always the first to jump off the tracks. It only takes the lead machine getting sideways to throw hundreds of cars in tow into complete disaster, as they accordion into each other, typically accompanied by a massive fireball for good measure.

Life isn't a whole lot different for us. Sometimes all it takes is a pebble on the tracks of life to smash up the whole train behind us.

I think it's time to look at what could potentially be keeping us from both an authentic relationship with other men and with Jesus Christ. And since we now know how critical our legacy is, we absolutely must get past the "analysis paralysis" that is keeping us perpetually in "park." The next chapters are going to hit on the usual suspects—and some not so usual ones as well—that can throw our train off of the rails in a hurry.

Although I am more of the traditional action movie/cop show kind of guy, I am also very much a fan of the *Pirates of the Caribbean* movie series. Jack Sparrow is a brilliant character, and for some reason I just think Captain Barbossa is also off the chain. And, probably like most of you, I often feel as if the original of any movie can rarely be outdone by its respective sequel, and the *Pirates* franchise is no different... *The Curse of the Black Pearl is*, and always will be, the best installment in the series.

Not to belabor the plot or to accidentally be a spoiler for the one man on earth who has yet to see it, but *The Curse of the Black Pearl* is a classic good guy/bad guy flick. Captain Barbossa and his crew of miscreants have been cursed by a chest full of gold doubloons buried by Cortez (and stolen by Barbossa), and the only way the curse can be broken is by returning all 882 pieces back to the chest. And, as it turns out, Elizabeth Swann has the last remaining gold coin, which she wears as necklace. She has found herself at the dinner table aboard the Black Pearl vessel with a very undead Captain Barbossa. He flashes the gold at Elizabeth, whom he believes to be the only child of fellow pirate "Bootstrap Bill" Turner, and a conversation ensues:

Barbossa: You don't know what this is, do ye?

Elizabeth: It's a pirate medallion.

Barbossa: This is Aztec gold. One of 882 identical pieces they delivered in a stone chest to Cortez himself. Blood money paid to stem the slaughter he wreaked upon them with his armies. But the greed of Cortez was insatiable, so the heathen gods placed upon the gold a terrible curse. Any mortal that removes but a single piece from that stone chest shall be punished... for eternity.

Elizabeth: I hardly believe in ghost stories anymore, Captain Barbossa

Barbossa: Aye. That's exactly what I thought when we were first told the tale. Buried on an island of dead what cannot be found except for those who know where it is. Find it, we did. There be the chest. Inside be the gold. And we took 'em all. We spent 'em and traded 'em and frittered 'em away on drink and food and pleasurable company. The more we gave them away, the more we came to realize that the drink would not satisfy, food turned to ash in our mouths, and all the pleasurable company in the world could not slake our lust. We are cursed men, Miss Turner. Compelled by greed, we were, but now we are consumed by it.

When I first heard the dialogue between Barbossa and Elizabeth, especially the last part of the captain's description of the curse, I was again reminded of men, specifically as it relates to the economy in which we are currently attempting to survive. We are cursed men, born with a sin nature thanks to a guy named Adam.

You know, the first decade of this new millennium has been brutal on the bank account, to say the least. The words "global economic meltdown" have been used all too often to illustrate exactly what has happened all around us. In just a few short years, literally tens of thousands of jobs have ended. Credit card defaults are at an all-time high; 20% of credit card bills are no longer being paid, as men are faced with the choice of putting food on the table or paying down revolving debt. Foreclosures are at record levels, as people find themselves with loans they are unable to repay, while the value of their homes plummet. Even the price of gasoline flirts occasionally with the $5 per gallon mark, which further hammers us.

The news claims millions of people of people have been somehow affected by this economy; and, given its cyclical nature, we can only assume that, regardless of when you happen to be reading this book, there is a strong probability feasting and famine will continue to be bedfellows.

Every day, countless men wake up wondering if they will ever find a job, while others have downgraded their employment, taking whatever comes their way to ensure survival to whatever the degree.

The good news in all of this is that God is still on the throne. Although it may not seem like it in the midst of economic devastation, He is entirely good and faithful, and we are going to make it.

As I have not only watched but also lived through a horrible set of economic circumstances, I have narrowed the "victims" of the meltdown to two types of men.

The first is the "Financial Suicide" guy. He's the one who got a little a carried away and is now in the throes of the consequences of a series of "not so good" financial decisions. In the early 2000s, I was involved in the real estate industry in Florida, and I stood by as men invested in homes. Lots of homes. In one case, a man I know took out a $60,000 equity line on his home to buy six new investment homes. During the height of the feeding frenzy in Florida, homes that were half-completed were reselling for double, and his plan was to sell all six homes prior to closing. Unfortunately, the market crashed and the investor ended up "holding the bag" with six homes he couldn't unload. He ultimately ended up going through not six but seven foreclosures as he lost his first home due to non-payment.

The second is the "Innocent Victim" guy. This is the guy who had nothing to do with the job loss or the subsequent challenges that came along with it. He's sort of like that person walking along a sidewalk when a roadside bomb explodes. It wasn't his car, it wasn't his bomb, and it wasn't his fault… but he stills gets killed. Men who have seen jobs evaporate as companies close are initiated into this group. They're just collateral damage.

On top of that, the Innocent Victim guy may have also even lived his life as a disciple and has really done everything "right" (at least as right as we can as a fallen man), but he still ended up getting blown out of the water.

If I was to put myself into a category, it would have to be the "Financial Suicide" guy, and I would be willing to bet if you have ever had more money than you actually need, you may be there also. It's amazing how unreliant we suddenly become on our Lord when we have everything we want. Often, it's just a shell game and it takes a while for the reality of the decision(s) to impact us, but it invariably catches us.

In Ecclesiastes, Solomon unpacks a series of things that, in plain English, are just a flat out a waste of time. And since Solomon has been tapped as the wisest man ever, this is worth considering as we continue to march on:

First, he pretty much calls everything we dwell on "meaningless." The word "meaningless" is even called "vanity" in the King James Version of the Bible, so you can be sure it's just useless no matter how you slice it. In no particular order, Solomon calls pleasure, folly, and even toil "meaningless." We work all day only to leave it behind for someone else.

Then he really hits home when he calls wisdom itself "meaningless." Have you ever met a person who continues to go back to school decade after decade to add more initials to their growing list of academic accolades? First it's a bachelor's degree, then a master's, then a doctorate. Granted, some do it for career advancement, but I have met men who continue to chase down more education as a way to validate their lives (which may be due to the "story" they believe about themselves, like "I am stupid" or "I'll never amount to anything").

But, Solomon puts this pursuit of knowledge like this:

Then I applied myself to the understanding of wisdom, and also of madness and folly, but I learned that this, too, is a chasing after the wind. For with much wisdom comes much sorrow; the more knowledge, the more grief

Ecclesiastes 1:17-18

Without really excluding much of anything, Solomon calls everything we burn up hours on as a "chasing after the wind." Obviously, catching the wind is not really a possibility, but in the unlikely event you are fast enough to do so, you still only end up with a big handful of air. It's a loser either way. Remember what Captain Barbossa said?

"...Drink would not satisfy, food turned to ash in our mouths, and all the pleasurable company in the world could not slake our lust."

That's pirate talk for a chasing after the wind!

I've spent my fair share of days chasing all kinds of wind. Of course, at the time it seemed like I was on the right track. It was 2004, and everything seemed to be hitting on all cylinders. I had a great job as a new homes sales person, was soon to be joyfully remarried, and had people lining up to buy homes. And to make it even more incredible, my boss decided to give me one of the two positions at our upcoming community, which was sure to be a major coup in the real estate market.

I remember, multiple times, doing the commission math with my sales partner and getting lost in the dollar signs. It started to consume me as the grand opening date got closer and closer. And guys, the bottom line here was the bottom line. If we were going to sell 72 homes at an average sales price of $750,000 and I was going to get 1% commission, then I was looking at something like $30,000 per month over 18 months. And we knew they were going to fly off the shelf primarily because the Florida market was so hot. We had more than 4,000 prospective buyers who had already called from the sign in front of the bare dirt, so it was going to be like shooting fish in a barrel.

So I started spending money I didn't have. I paid off a credit card with a massive balance using the equity line from our home because our home had increased in value from $210,000 to over $430,000. And, after all, I was going to be making $30,000 soon, right? My wife (aka, the voice of the Lord) kept saying, "I need to see it to believe it," but I just reassured her it was all perfect. You know, she never bought the deal and lived far more sensibly than I wanted to.

Then came a series of mishaps (to put it mildly) with regard to the neighborhood release. The first challenge came calling as a legal issue. No, it was not some major zoning violation or building on a protected wetland but rather the simple word "the." Apparently someone had drafted the contract as "The Residences at University Groves," and the county informed us we couldn't start the neighborhood name with "the." So the county sent the documents back asking they all be re-written as "Residences at University Groves, The." Seriously? Bad went to worse when the papers never moved off of the attorney's desk, as he was no longer with the firm and no one looked in his stack of papers.

The clincher came with our lakefront homesites. If you know anything about Florida real estate, "waterfront" or "lakefront" lots are built by simply digging a big hole in the middle and using the backfill to build up the sites. The hole consequently fills up with water, and PRESTO, instant lake. Unfortunately, the developer dug a bit too deep and the resulting dirt that we used to level the homesites tipped the radon meter. As a result, we were unable to build on the lots until we removed the top 18 inches of soil, trucked it off of the property, and replaced it with clean dirt. The net result of the aforementioned delays was almost a year. And, during that time, the real estate market made a radical shift (actually it just died where it was standing) and all 4,000 people on my "sure thing" list evaporated.

But the debt I had mounted didn't. What's worse, our home value plummeted back to $210,000, so the equity was a just a fiscal fantasy as well. I was trying to live like a millionaire and paid a heavy price for it. And we never did see any of that money.

The whole debacle reminds me of a scene from the movie *Over the Hedge*, which is yet another computer animated masterpiece that stars the voice of none other than my hero, Bruce Willis, as RJ the Raccoon. It's the dead of winter, and RJ is starving. In fact, he gets so hungry he ends up trying to smash through the plate glass front of a vending machine with a golf club in an attempt to score some candy. Just as he is about to swing, he spots the cave of his hibernating bear friend, Vincent.

Devising a scheme to rob the bear of some of his food stash, RJ sneaks into the cave. And right before he catapults himself over the bear with an inflatable raft, he quietly reminds himself, "Only take what you need. Only take what you need." The next scene you see is of RJ standing atop a gigantic pile of food on a Red Rider wagon, as he has hijacked every bit of Vincent's winter food supply. And he would have gotten away unscathed had it not been for a can of "Spuddies" potato chips that quickly wakes the bear up when RJ vents the can. Ultimately, after having his life threatened, RJ accidentally pushes the grocery-packed wagon down a hill, where every bit of food is destroyed by an oncoming semi truck.

"Only take what you need." I really wish, during the real estate season of my life, someone had said, "Hey, are you sure you need to be living like this?" But alas, I just spent it all before I even earned it.

As a result, I learned a valuable lesson about stewardship and also what Paul meant when he said:

> *I am not saying this because I am in need, for I have learned to be content whatever the circumstances. I know what it is to be in need, and I know what it is to have plenty. I have learned the secret of being content in any and every situation, whether well fed or hungry, whether living in plenty or in want.*

> *Philippians 4:11-12*

God truly does have a sense of humor. After all, he took a guy making money in the previously lucrative real estate field and dropped him headlong into full-time ministry. I felt like I was in an irreversible jam, even quietly contemplating bankruptcy more than a few times. But somehow, after a whole lot of repentance peppered with the occasional terror of not being able to pay the bills at all, God has gotten me through it relatively undamaged. Somehow I even managed to avert bankruptcy.

If you are one of those "Oops, I shot myself in the foot" guys, like I obviously appear to be, then step one is to just make a change. I put my family in a pretty precarious position financially, and it sure didn't help when the housing market slid backwards. And the money bomb detonated. But it's never too late to change or to pray for a speedy recovery. Yes, we're likely going to have some consequences from making bad choices, like receiving the inevitable "800" number calls from angry people who want their money. But God is faithful, and we are going to make it.

While not often preached on, the books of Judges, Kings, and Chronicles all show us just how faithful God can be when just one man has a change of heart.

Remember that Israel was caught in a cycle of sin and repentance, often turning back to the gods of the other people and worshiping idols, Asherah poles, and even what were known as "high places"—altars to other gods that were in, well, high places. One of the problems both Judah and Israel (the kingdoms were divided at this point) continued to have was an issue with what is often called "partial obedience." A king would repent for his nation, tear down the idols, and cut down the Asherah poles. But time and time again, the Bible reads, "But the high places remained." These guys would have a change of heart but hang on to the high places for some reason. So if you plan on making a change, go all the way and hold nothing back. Leave it all on the field, so to speak. Partial obedience is simply disobedience.

Check out the following four successive generations of the Kings of Judah:

King Hezekiah - His father, Ahaz, did not do what was right in the eyes of the Lord and even sacrificed his own son. But Hezekiah worshipped and followed the Lord God. The Bible says there was no one like him before or after. He tore down the Asherah poles and false idols and all of the high places in Judah. This guy is cool, as God even gave him 15 more years to live after praying for God's intervention against the king of Assyria.

King Manasseh - Son of King Hezekiah who took over after his father died. He did evil in the eyes of the Lord and even rebuilt all of the stuff his dad had torn down, including the high places that were so hard to get rid of in the first place. This guy brought a lot of pain to Judah and shed a lot of blood, too.

King Amon - Son of King Manasseh. This guy did it just like his dad, and God was not happy about it. He only lasted two years.

King Josiah - Son of Amon who became king at eight years old (never underestimate a kid). He did what was right and even rediscovered the Word of God (aka, Book of the Law).

He presented it to Judah and made a call for all-out repentance. He went back and tore down all the idols his grandfather Manasseh had put back up. When he tore down the high places, Josiah even went into the tribes of Israel and tore theirs down, too.

The cycle of sin and repentance illustrated by the Kings of Judah reveals to us we can indeed play a vital role in changing our situation. In my case, I just had to learn to live within my means, without credit cards or deferred payments. These days, if I can't buy it with cash, I'm not buying it. The credit cards are plastic shrapnel in the garbage can, and we live within our means as best we can.

A word of caution if you are battling a bad financial run and have yet to pull the plug on bad habits. God is faithful to us when we scream, "Hey God, I made a wrong turn! Help!" But for those of us who are a little more stubborn, He has been known to take matters into His own hands from time to time. After all, He is the creator of the universe, so He can pretty much do anything He must in order to get our attention or to even break a cycle of bad decisions.

In 1 Samuel 5, the Philistines (the same people where good old Goliath came from) have managed to steal the ark of the Covenant. As Indiana Jones describes it, the ark is "the chest the Hebrews used to carry the Ten Commandments around in… the actual Ten Commandments. The original stone tablets that Moses brought down out of Mount Horeb and smashed." Having snagged the most important weapon from the Israelites, the Philistines decide to put the ark in the temple of their "god" named "Dagon." Since Dagon was THE god of the Philistines, you can be certain the room was likely pretty well guarded. But that didn't stop God from handling the theft:

Then they carried the ark into Dagon's temple and set it beside Dagon. When the people of Ashdod rose early the next day, there was Dagon, fallen on his face on the ground before the ark of the Lord! They took Dagon and put him back in his place. But the following morning when they rose, there was Dagon, fallen on his face on the ground before the ark of the Lord! His head and hands had been broken off and were lying on the threshold; only his body remained.

1 Samuel 5:2-4

Can you imagine? After the first night in the room with the ark, Dagon ends up face-down on the floor. No one entered or left that room, but God pushed him over anyway. The next day, whoever was in charge of Dagon's room was probably a little stunned. I envision the Philistine guard standing little Dagon back up (I have always assumed Dagon looks like the little gold statue at the beginning of *Raiders of the Lost Ark* for some reason), brushing the dirt off of his face, and locking the room. The next day, the same guard comes back in to find Dagon broken into a bunch of pieces. After that, the Philistines made a plan to get the ark out of their country before it killed them all. God can, and sometimes will, break us in order change us.

As you also may have noticed in the lives of King Amon and King Manasseh, bad decisions are epidemic and can go from generation to generation. But so can a legacy of doing right in the eyes of God, as we see with Hezekiah and Josiah. It only takes one guy to trigger a chain of events that can change it all. Like

Josiah and many other kings who knew the right thing to do, we can play an active role in changing how our legacy looks, even if we've made a mess of our finances. All we do is turn to God, pray for forgiveness, and let Him push the holy reset button.

But what if you weren't responsible for the financial state in your home? Maybe you were just standing on the sidewalk when the financial crisis bomb went off and you got taken out? The next chapter addresses the innocent victim of the economy.

Activation Questions

- *To what level have I been impacted by the latest economic crisis?*

- *Are there any parts of my lifestyle that could be classified as bad stewardship?*

- *To what extent do I use borrowed money, and would I say the outstanding balance is "living within my means"?*

- *What lifestyle changes could I make to ensure survival if things get worse financially?*

19.

COLLATERAL DAMAGE
(When the Financial Crisis Hits Home)

Apparently like most of the people in the USA these days, I have taken to watching reality TV shows. While I refuse to watch programs about teen moms or a bunch of drunk kids living in a million dollar house on an island, I do like shows like *Survivor*, where the last man standing wins and *Auction Hunters*, the show where two men bid on abandoned storage units and find amazing hidden treasures. Another one of my favorites is called *Bomb Patrol Afghanistan*, which follows a US Navy Explosives Ordnance Disposal team as they find and dismantle IEDs, or Improvised Explosive Devices, along desert roads while downrange in the Middle East. This show is especially close to my heart, as my dad was a Navy EOD guy; although in his era they were disarming limpet mines and other underwater bombs. Now the Navy EOD teams are nowhere near water.

I read an article a few days ago, as our involvement in both Iraq and Afghanistan continues, about roadside bombs. These aren't the IEDs buried under roads for some unsuspecting armored vehicle to run over but rather the kind placed in cars parked alongside roads. This type of "warfare," which is used by cowards for the most part, involves detonating a bomb in the trunk of a car with the intent being to kill as many innocent bystanders as possible. Dozens of these bombs go off every week in nations all over the world, and hundreds of nearby people lose their lives as a result.

Right here in the United States, we've experienced roadside explosives in a much grander scale in the past. In 1995, two men triggered an explosion in front of the Alfred P. Murrah Federal building in Oklahoma City, Oklahoma, which resulted in 168 deaths, including 19 children under the age of six, with an additional 680 injured. On top of that, 324 buildings within a 16-block radius were destroyed or damaged, and 86 cars were burned up. One bomb in a rental truck did damage that permanently affected an otherwise peaceful midwestern town.

Similarly, the severe economic downturn in 2007 did the same thing, figuratively speaking, to families all over the world. Construction-related industries were obviously hit hardest, as once salespeople stopped selling homes, there was nothing to build. Tradesmen and suppliers were closing in Florida and in other "hot" real estate markets every day. Personally, I watched the largest roofing contractor in my state, Florida, shut its doors, forcing the owner to move to another state to get a job as a salesman.

This kind of financial crisis isn't limited to 2007, as we saw even greater devastation on Black Monday in 1929, when Wall Street crashed, and also witnessed it on a lesser scale soon after the Tax Reform Act of 1986. Rest assured this isn't the first and likely won't be the last financial situation that results in widespread collateral damage.

As I have traveled, I have listened to countless men tell of financial ruin in spite of honoring God in every part of their lives. I mean, these dudes read, pray, tithe, love, and serve like apostles but are still hard hit. If you are one of those men, I want to call your attention to our Lord, Jesus Christ. Would you agree Jesus was perfect and led a sinless life? For 33 years, Jesus didn't even sin, which puts Him light years ahead of even the best men we know here on earth. Perfect while being both fully God and fully man, Jesus lived a flawless life and suffered death for our sins, not His. With all this taken into consideration, look at the beginning of the Gospel of Mark:

> *At that time Jesus came from Nazareth in Galilee and was baptized by John in the Jordan. As Jesus was coming up out of the water, he saw heaven being torn open and the Spirit descending on him like a dove. And a voice came from heaven: "You are my Son, whom I love; with you I am well pleased." At once the Spirit sent him out into the desert, and he was in the desert forty days, being tempted by Satan*
>
> *Mark 1:9-12a*

Immediately after our sinless Savior was baptized and God Himself spoke of who He was, Jesus was sent into the desert for 40 days so he could get hammered on by Satan. And Jesus didn't even do anything wrong! His circumstances took an immediate strange and not so pleasant turn, and Jesus never sinned, either on the front or the back end of that month-long jaunt into the desert. Now I don't know about you, but if it was good enough for Jesus, then we should hold our heads high if we get to share in bad situations while trying to do good. Persecution is part of the enlistment package, and financial trials are no exception.

So if you happen to be that man who got caught in the fiscal crossfire, I want to encourage you. First, get connected to another man and tell him what's going on. Be honest with him so he knows what and how to pray for you and your family. Secondly, know that God didn't get caught blindsided by what's happening financially either in your home or the world. God didn't turn to Jesus and say, "Whoa, I didn't see that one coming." In fact, God even spells out just who He is and His level of involvement in our challenges in Isaiah:

> *I form the light and create darkness, I bring prosperity and create disaster; I, the Lord, do all these things*
>
> *Isaiah 45:7*

But God, who is still on the throne, goes on to say:

> *"For a brief moment I abandoned you, but with deep compassion I will bring you back. In a surge of anger I hid my face from you for a moment, but with everlasting kindness I will have compassion on you," says the Lord your Redeemer*
>
> *Isaiah 54:7-8*

In light of those two Scriptures from the prophet Isaiah, we all need to keep two promises close at hand that my friend, Patrick Morley, pointed out so well in his book *How to Survive the Economic Meltdown*:

1. God is in charge. He has a plan. He was not surprised or somehow caught off guard by this meltdown. God is not sitting up in heaven wringing His hands about how this will turn out. He is altogether good and trustworthy. God is sovereignly orchestrating all of the seemingly random circumstances in your life.

2. You're going to get through this. Yes, you will have to go through it. There are no shortcuts. And yes, you can't know how it will turn out. That belongs to the realm of God's will. And yes, it is going to take some time. But you will get through this.

That whole "no shortcut" thing is a real killer. There aren't any fast ways around it, nor can we avoid the valley altogether. In fact, in Psalm 23, King David clearly speaks of being in the "valley of the shadow of death" himself but confirms that he won't fear evil because God is right there in that valley with him. As He is with us to this day.

As conditions worsen for some men, I have been asked some tough questions about the nature of God. I hear things like "how can this happen to me?" and "is it God's will that I suffer like this and lose my house?" Sometimes I am tempted to answer them the same way Father Cavanaugh answers "Rudy" Ruettiger when the kid asks if God is going to hear his prayers: "Son," Father Cavanaugh says, "in 35 years of religious study, I've come up with only two hard, incontrovertible facts: there is a God, and I'm not Him." I hate to tell men I have no idea why bad things sometimes happen to good people, but I don't know much about God or His will. With a little digging, however, I did discover something interesting about God's will.

There are actually two different types of "God's will," as far as I can surmise. One is His "perfect" will, while the other is His "permissive" will. There's a huge difference between the two, and it can be best illustrated by looking into the first two kings of Israel. During the time of the judges, prior to the kings, the nation of Israel gets a little antsy with the way the whole judge system works. As they survey all of their neighboring nations, a common denominator emerges: all of the nations, except Israel, have a king. So the people of Israel begin to complain to God about it, and as a result, God taps Samuel with the mission of securing the first-ever king of Israel. You may recall this King was named Saul, and he ultimately blew it through a series of bad decisions that culminated with him losing the favor of God. King Saul was, by definition, God's permissive will. The people moaned and griped enough that God finally gave them what they wanted. And they got King Saul.

On the other hand, if you were to ask God Himself who His PERFECT will was for King of Israel, it was King David. Even as a boy, David was a man after God's own heart. From the minute he popped Goliath in the head with that rock to the end of his reign, David was God's choice for the nation of Israel.

Sometimes, in our frantic rush to ascertain God's will, we ask and ask until I believe God finally just says, "Fine! You want that huge house? Here ya go!" For all we know, His perfect will may be a mission trip to Nicaragua, but we push it until we get it. And the crazy thing about God's permissive will is we still ultimately end up with His perfect will anyway. Sure, Saul was a pit stop created by a lot of whining, but Israel eventually got David because that's what God wanted.

So often, I think this fast food culture we live in has caused us to fall prey to the tyranny of the urgent, and we make decisions that just end up costing us precious time. I often wonder if my overspending delayed my emergence into ministry. Even to this day, it impacts our personal finances, which can preclude us from following His leading... simply because we don't have the money.

So is personal financial worry the rock that threw your train off the tracks? I know that, whether you played a role in the state of you personal finances or not, it doesn't make the potential wall between you and God any less impending. Maybe you feel unworthy to re-engage because you somehow think God is condemning you for some bad decisions. Or perhaps you're just so frustrated by circumstances beyond your control that you've all but checked out. Both are understandable, but both are also a lie.

For whatever reason, we are where we are financially. Maybe it was a self-inflicted wallet wound, or maybe it was just friendly fire. But when, not if, God gets us through this one, we will once again be able to guide another man through the same valley in the future. We just have to tell them about it and how God ultimately pulled through for us yet again.

Activation Questions

- *How has the state of the economy affected my life? Foreclosure? Job loss?*

- *Was I forced to downgrade careers due to a job loss?*

- *How has my faith been impacted by what has happened financially?*

20

THIS IS JEOPARDY!
(The Three-Letter S Word)

Every so often, my wife and I end up watching *Jeopardy*, usually just to see how many answers we don't know. I'm always blown away by how much information some of the contestants have packed away in their brains. Were it not for *Wheel of Fortune* coming on right before *Jeopardy*, I would feel pretty stupid. It's funny just how different both of those shows are and how markedly different the contestants are. For example, *Wheel* will have a puzzle using a Jack Nicholson quote, and someone will answer with a deliberately slow tempo, "You… can't… handle… the… PORCH!" It's then that I feel some slight academic redemption since I actually know the answer and they don't! Then we move on to *Jeopardy*, where the answer is in the form of a question, and you arrive just in time to hear, "Who is Bernardo O'Higgins?" I believe there is no other place in TV land where you can feel so smart and so dumb all in the same hour!

Years ago, Joni and I were again sitting down to *Jeopardy* and it was College Night. There were three young students, each dressed in their respective college sweatshirts. One was from Harvard, one was from Yale, and one was from Brown, so suffice it to say I was going to go "0 for life" on this show. The first board (the one with the easy questions at the beginning) popped up, and one of the categories was "Three-Letter Words." "How hard can that be?" I thought to myself. The first question, or answer, showed up at the top of the category and Alex Trebek read, "According to St. Paul, what did Adam bring into the world that Jesus took out?"

Sitting right next to us was our then eight-year-old boy, Daniel. "SIN!" he yelled. "What is SIN!" Even an eight-year-old was faster on the draw than I was when it came to *Jeopardy*, and Danny beat me soundly. Then, from the television, came silence. There sat three completely dumbfounded Ivy League college students who had no idea what sin was or how the Word of God described it. And I don't think these kids are alone.

How often do we really think about the whole concept of sin? As men, our natural reaction at this point would be to turn to the next chapter or stop reading this stupid book, but hang with me for a minute. After all, this whole sin thing can bring any forward momentum we have to a dead stop in a hurry. And since most of us don't have that Jonathan guy in our lives to encourage, support, and—in this case—tell us we're being an idiot, we just keep re-living the same issues over and over again. Eventually, it kills us or kills something around us that really matters. No matter how hard we try to bury it or hide it or even break from a cycle of sin, it is resilient, to say the least.

I am a big fan of the *Oceans* movie franchise, specifically *Ocean's Eleven*, mostly because of the all-star cast. Some of you older guys may remember the 1960 "Rat Pack" version featuring Dean Martin, Sammy Davis, Jr., Peter Lawford and Frank Sinatra; but I am alluding to the more recent movie starring George Clooney, Matt Damon, and Brad Pitt. The movie involves a casino heist where Danny Ocean and a group of talented teammates decide to steal $150 million during a boxing match. That would obviously be a slamdunk case of sin, but that would be too easy to illustrate, so I want to focus on how these guys pull off the initial penetration of the casino's seemingly impenetrable security system.

Ocean and his crew determine the best way to shut down the casino's security system is to kill all of the power on the Las Vegas Strip at once. To some, that would seem impossible, but the men overcome the daunting task by creating a device intended to emit an EMP, or electo-magnetic pulse. Detonated at the correct time, they figure the power will be interrupted for roughly 30 seconds, which will be just long enough for Ocean to break through the laser triggers in the hotel. The plan goes off without a hitch, other than destroying the van that the EMP unit was hidden in, and Ocean (George Clooney) and Linus (Matt Damon) succeed in breaking into the safe.

While the break-in is cool to witness, the most shocking thing about this particular scene is what happens throughout the casino during that 30 seconds of total darkness. While the film's focus is on the break-in when the lights are off, the cameras shift back to the casino and the boxing ring when the lights come back on. And it is, to say the least, chaotic. People are climbing over the tops of Blackjack tables in order to snatch a handful of chips, the boxers are attempting to kill each other in the ring, and other folks are breaking into slot machines. It is an amazing visual illustration of just how quickly we jeopardize our integrity when the lights are out.

If you have been in the church for longer than a week, you have likely heard "integrity" is defined as what we do when no one is looking. It's who we are when we are away from home or when we are all alone. We have an amazing capability of wearing a mask when we are in front of other people, but it's who we are when we are by ourselves that defines our character. Thanks to Adam, the first guy ever, we are shackled with sin from the very second we are born. The Psalmist nails it by saying:

Surely I was sinful at birth, sinful from the time my mother conceived me

Psalm 51:5

Even from birth the wicked go astray; from the womb they are wayward and speak lies

Psalm 58:3

Thanks, Adam! From the day we fall out of the womb, we are destined to sin. I once heard someone say you never have to train a toddler to lie, but you do have to train truth into them. And, even as adults, we men flirt with disaster every day. And, to make matters worse, we somehow have deluded ourselves into thinking God is just as blind when we are alone as everyone else is. Heads up, men. We have Audience of One, and He sees it all, whether we like it or not. During His Sermon on the Mount, Jesus speaks of acting out our righteousness before men, giving to the poor without drawing attention to ourselves, and even praying in a closet. And there is a very consistent theme:

Then your Father, who sees what is done in secret, will reward you

Matthew 6:4b

God sees everything that is done in secret, and the antithesis of "reward" is probably not too pretty. If we continue to push the edge of the envelope, then we run the inevitable risk of getting found out:

> *For there is nothing hidden that will not be disclosed, and nothing concealed that will not be known or brought out into the open*
>
> *Luke 8:17*

In other words, it's not a question of "if" God is ultimately going to snag us but "when." And the collateral damage isn't worth the risk. Ever.

I made a commitment to myself, prior to writing about the "S" word, that I wouldn't get all pious and holy, mainly because I am in no place to throw rocks at anybody. Not a day goes by where I don't say something I regret, think something that is less than kind about the dude driving in front of me, and even cast sideways remarks at my very own brothers in Christ. I also know when conditions are the best for me to get way off my Jesus game.

Since we are now all sitting here, doing a review of just how far off we can be from the will of God, it's actually better if we collectively figure out how to sink this sin boat in which we are all floating around. Recognizing the triggers is always a good start, and there is a relatively easy acronym of "red flag" situations that will help to keep us out of trouble.

HALT

No, I don't mean stop reading. That's the acronym. We men are more likely to sin when we encounter the four triggers represented in the word "HALT."

The "H" is for hungry. How reasonable is any man when he's hungry? Our tempers get short, our patience runs out quicker, and when this happens we tend to yell or even have a tantrum like a kid.

The "A" is for angry. When we are ticked off, we are far more likely to punch a wall or yell. I used to love working on my car back in high school. It was a little Toyota, and I could take the whole engine apart if I needed to. It had a carburetor, points, and a bunch of stuff they just don't put in cars any more. One time, the car wouldn't idle correctly and would stall at literally every traffic light. I cleaned the carb and checked the ignition and it still died. Then I replaced the plugs, points, condenser, distributor cap, rotor, and even the spark plug wires. And it still died. Frustrated, I beat the carburetor to death with a hammer, which cost a few hundred dollars to replace. And even with the new carburetor, it still died. As it turned out, it was a small 20-amp fuse under the dashboard marked "engine" that was the culprit. A lousy 50-cent fuse! Anger always carries a cost with it, because some sin will follow.

The "L" is for lonely. I will go into this in greater detail in the next chapter, but let's just say the Internet can be the downfall of many a good man if he gets lonely. There's a reason, I believe, it's called the World Wide Web. It can grab you from a million different angles, and it's nearly impossible to get out of most of the time.

The "T" is for tired. Just like when we're hungry, being tired can make the fuse a little shorter and burn a little faster.

Now that we have some sin triggers, the obvious next step is to figure out how to increase detonation time. If you're hungry, take the time to eat. The world isn't going to fall apart around you if you take time to eat. In fact, you will be much healthier and your metabolism will correct itself. Don't allow yourself to skip meals.

If you're tired, take a look at sleep patterns. Make sure that you are incorporating rest into your daily regimen, and try and get at least six hours of sleep at night. As hard as it can be, figure out a way to shut the brain down. I tend to wake up in problem solving mode, and some guys go to sleep that way.

The remaining two, being lonely and being angry, don't have solutions that are nearly as simple as the previous ones. This is where having a wingman can really help you succeed, because this guy can help you address the issues, talk you off the ledge, and even prevent the inevitable sin as a result.

Don't allow yourself to get lonely. Make a covenant with a man to connect with you if you are in hotel rooms or on the road frequently. There is nothing more comforting than getting a phone call asking how you're doing when you are miles from home. Sometimes, just asking "what are you thinking about?" or "what are you watching on TV?" can create a safety net. If, while alone, the TV or the Internet slowly draws you into a place you'd rather not be, pull the plug. Literally. Don't log on, and don't turn the TV on. Call your back up and talk through the day.

And when anger hits, disengage. A dogfight can quickly turn into a one-plane air show if the other plane checks out of the fight. Whether it's at work or at home, keep your wingman's number on speed dial. Talk it through with him, pray it through, and stay cool. Don't storm out of the room or swing at the wall. It could save your carburetor or your marriage.

Finally, we would be missing the bigger picture if I fail to mention the most important aspect of the sin battle. His name is Jesus Christ. Maybe it's been a while since you've really experienced Him. With all of the junk we men have to deal with, from money to marriages, Jesus sometimes gets lost in the mess somewhere.

But if you're doing battle alone with hidden sin, Jesus is truly the only answer. Sure, we can modify our behavior and even solicit the aid of a guy to lay down some serious cover fire for us, but at the end of the day, Jesus has already won the battle. So before we get into the "why" of where we drove off the road, let's reconnect with Jesus, who can put us back on the road.

Maybe it's the first time or the first time in a long time, but we all need to be grounded in our Savior. Remember that, when Jesus took the nails in His hands and feet, He took all of our sin away. Past sin, present sin, and even future sin was removed once and for all. So do me a favor. Find a quiet place and make a supernatural phone call to Jesus:

> Lord Jesus, I need You, Lord. No matter how hard I try to do it right, I still fail. I am a sinner and I need Your salvation. Jesus, I ask that You come into my heart and save me. Thank You for dying on the cross, and thank You for saving me. Thank You for loving me. I want to live my life for You and serve You every day of my life.
>
> Amen

You are a soldier in God's army. With Jesus living in us, we are given an exit strategy from sin, and with His Holy Spirit living in us, addictions, desires, and sin patterns can be crushed. It doesn't mean we won't get our tails kicked by sin, but saying that prayer does mean we will spend eternity in heaven with Jesus. The next step is to go to war against sin with Jesus as our point man and our rear guard. Grab your wingman, and tell him what's going on and go to war because:

For where two or three come together in my name, there am I with them

Matthew 18:20

Please don't continue to live life as if no one is watching. God wants the best for us, and if we keep living a life that isn't all He wants for us, He will get involved and He will eventually correct our course deviation.

Activation Questions

- *When do I find myself most likely to do something stupid (also known as "sin")?*

- *Do I live my life the same way, whether alone or with some-one else? Is what they see truly what they get?*

- *Did I connect, or re-connect with Jesus by praying the Prayer of Salvation in this chapter? If so, I need to tell a few guys about it so they can keep me covered!*

21

THE FIFTH COMPARTMENT
(When the Course Is Compromised)

APRIL 15, 1912, marks an epic battle between man's ego and God.

The luxury cruise ship, *Titanic*, was built in Belfast, North Ireland, by the shipbuilding company "Harland and Wolff." A man named Lord Pirrie, who was a friend of Bruce Ismay, the managing director of the White Star Line, owned the company. The chief designer of the Titanic was Ismay's son-in-law, Thomas Andrews.

When construction of the Titanic began in 1909, Harland and Wolff had to make substantial alterations to their shipyard (including larger piers and gantries) to accommodate their twin giant liners, *Titanic* and her sister ship *Olympic*. The two ships were to be built side-by-side, with *Olympic*'s maiden voyage falling under the command of Captain Edward Smith, who also piloted *Titanic* to its demise.

The Titanic was constructed with 16 watertight compartments, and each compartment had doors that were designed to close automatically if the water level rose above a certain height. Believe it or not, considering the relatively primitive engineering advancements of the age, these doors could be electronically closed from the bridge. Because of this technology, *Titanic* was theoretically able to stay afloat if any two compartments or the first four became flooded. Shortly after *Titanic* hit the iceberg, it was revealed that the first five compartments were flooded, while a sixth one was breached. The total cost of the RMS *Titanic* was $7.5 million (in 1912)

I can't imagine that anyone in 1912 believed nearly 35 tons of steel could be unsinkable, but for some reason, there were an awful lot of people who did. It's funny because even the shipbuilders themselves insisted that the *Titanic* was never advertised as an "unsinkable" ship. They claim that the "unsinkable" tagline was the result of articles published about the ship that grew into a delusion. And apparently, that myth of unsinkability grew even more after *Titanic* hit the bottom of the Atlantic.

Even the vice president of the White Star Line bought the story, because when he heard that the *Titanic* was in trouble, he publicly announced, "We place absolute confidence in the *Titanic*. We believe the boat is unsinkable." Since telecommunications weren't like they are today, the *Titanic* had already gone down by the time he uttered those words.

In the opinion of many, *Titanic* is still the worst maritime disaster in history. Of the 2,223 passengers and crew on board, only 706 survived. More than 1,500 people lost their lives on that night in 1912, and much of it had to do with men who pushed it a little too hard.

While movies like 1953's *A Night To Remember* have been made to depict the tragedy, James Cameron's 1997 version of *Titanic* is best, thanks to some significant upgrades in the arena of special effects. While it does occasionally masquerade itself as a "chick flick" with a fictional underlying love story, the movie captures both the disaster itself and the personalities of Ismay, Andrews, and Captain Smith with near precision.

Near the beginning of the film, we meet Caledon Hockley and his fiancé, Rose DeWitt Bukater, as they are ready to embark on the maiden voyage of *Titanic*. While Rose is unimpressed, her mother climbs out of the car and makes a bold statement, "So this is the ship they say is unsinkable." When Rose downplays the ship, Hockley is quick to jump to *Titanic's* defense, "It is unsinkable! God Himself could not sink this ship."

Oops. I am not a theologian nor am I the most learned Bible scholar by a long shot, but I do know Cal should have avoided bringing God into this. The apostle Paul puts it pretty clearly:

Do not be deceived: God cannot be mocked. A man reaps what he sows

Galatians 6:7

I'm not saying God heard Cal Hockley and decided to sink the *Titanic*, but I think we all need a friendly reminder of who owns everything we have been given, every idea we have come up with, and—frankly—every dollar we've made. Job said the Lord gives and the Lord takes away, so we need to tread lightly when we bring up a sovereign and holy God.

I received an interesting chain e-mail years ago that really emphasizes my point. Usually I just junk chain mails, as they ask me to send my bank account information to someone so I can inherit millions of dollars from my long-lost uncle in Nigeria, but for some reason I decided to hang on to this one. After doing a little research on the e-mail, I did discover some truth to some of the people mentioned.

John Lennon, of the Beatles, said in an interview in 1966, "Christianity will go. It will vanish and shrink. I needn't argue about that. I'm right and I will be proved right. We're more popular than Jesus now. I don't know which will go first—rock n' roll or Christianity." Fourteen years later, Lennon was shot dead by Mark David Chapman.

Bon Scott, the lead singer of the band AC/DC, sang the following lyrics in one of their popular rock songs, "Hey Momma, look at me I'm on my way to the promised land. I'm on the highway to hell." Scott died at 33 years of age after suffering from asphyxiation while intoxicated.

These are just two of the people mentioned in the e-mail, and it's pretty clear they flirted with disaster and died very early as a result. As men of God, we have to give credit where credit is due, and all of it goes to the Lord.

But I digress. Another scene in *Titanic* takes place at the captain's table during dinner, where Molly Brown asks Bruce Ismay if it was indeed his idea to name the ship *Titanic*. His reply illustrates just how confident he was in his handiwork, "Yes, actually. I wanted to convey sheer size. Size means stability, luxury, and—above all—strength." His very response shows just how overconfident the shipbuilder is, as if size makes the ship somehow indestructible.

Later, the ship slams into an iceberg, primarily because Captain Smith and Bruce Ismay decided to put the hammer down. The water is calm, the ship is flying, and to add insult to injury, the rudder on the ship is too small for the hull. In other words, since ships don't actually have brakes, they are doomed. But the helmsman does manage to turn the ship, resulting in the ice creating a large gash down the starboard bow of the Titanic. By the way, the general consensus is that, had they hit the iceberg head on, the giant ocean liner would have survived due to the construction of the watertight bulkheads in the bow of the ship.

With the ship at a dead stop, Ismay, Andrews, and the captain meet on the bridge to discuss the iceberg and the subsequent damage. Thomas Andrews proceeds to inform the other men that five compartments have been breached and the Titanic won't stay afloat regardless of whether they initiate the bilge pumps or not. In a complete state of shock, Bruce Ismay states, "This ship can't sink!"

In response, Thomas Andrews simply stares across the bridge at a dumbfounded Ismay and says, "It's made of iron, sir. I assure you she can. And she will. It's a mathematical certainty."

Can you imagine the shock Ismay and Captain Smith were hit with when told of the impending demise of the ship they had previously thought "unsinkable"? Their confidence in their magnificent ship was so solid that they had pushed it. Despite warnings of icebergs in the area and calm waters, the men had decided to crank up the last boilers to arrive in New York a day early. They had thrown caution to the wind, and the result was a disaster, literally.

Did you know that, statistically, only 12.5% of an iceberg is above the waterline? Sure, you can see the obvious chunk of ice floating in the water, but it's the 87.5% that can kill us. Just like the *Titanic*, it's the stuff we can't see that can take us out of the game.

Time and time again, men push it. After all, if no one sees us, what's the harm, right? We can even be blindly steaming along, with four of life's compartments already flooded. It's only when that fifth compartment floods that our entire life can sink. In the case of Tiger Woods, for example, that last text message spelled the end of his marriage. Like most of us, he kept pushing, until his fifth compartment spilled over the bulkhead.

The Bible puts the concept of the fifth compartment into one swift and convicting Scripture. As Moses is giving the Israelites advanced warning from God regarding their orders to take the Promised Land by force, if necessary, these words are spoken:

> *But if you fail to do this, you will be sinning against the LORD; and you may be sure that your sin will find you out*
>
> *Numbers 32:23*

There is another shipwreck that occurred on January 13, 2012. The story of the *Costa Concordia* can truly illustrate what I mean by "pushing it," comparing the grounding of the ship to the average man who puts his life and his marriage on the line.

The *Concordia* shipwreck is actually a real-life *Poseidon Adventure* that was plastered all over the media. Okay, maybe minus Gene Hackman, Ernest Borgnine, and a tidal wave, but the rescue operation was eerily familiar to the 1972 Irwin Allen disaster classic. For days, the *Costa Concordia* sat motionless at a 60-degree list, after blazing headlong into a reef off the coast of Isola del Giglio, Italy. As a result, at least 11 people died, a few dozen went missing, and rescuers spent countless hours blasting holes in the hull in an attempt to reach those who were missing out of the 4,200-plus passengers aboard. Amazingly, the ship was only hours into the cruise when the captain of the vessel, Francesco Schettino, decided to make a pass a little too close to the shoreline in an effort to "salute" a retired captain friend who lived on the nearby island. I guess we should call that "Fail #1" (by the way, the FPH—or "Fails Per Hour"—gets as epic as the *Titanic*).

Captain Schettino stated in an interview with investigators that he knew the waters well and had done it three or four times before but just ordered the turn "too late" (Yep, Fail #2). The ship's owners were reported as saying the maneuver was not authorized, and it was done solely at the Captain's discretion (Hello there, Fail #3). You have heard it said in many a cliché that the captain always goes down with his ship. Not this guy. Schettino jumped ship or, as he puts it, "fell into a life boat accidentally" (Really? That's Fail #4, if you are still keeping tabs). Then, when asked by the port officials to return to his ship to help the passengers, he declined. (BOOM! Fail #5.) I think if they look hard enough, Captain Schettino just may be responsible for the JFK assassination. On top of it all, the fine for a Captain abandoning his ship is 12 years in prison, not to mention the additional decades for multiple counts of involuntary manslaughter.

Ironically, a similar kind of shipwreck happens every day. Let's unpack this type of "shipwreck" in a different light, using the same "Fail" chronology as the *Costa* wreck. I will consolidate them, so you get what I am saying:

Fail #1 - Captain Schettino makes a pass too close to a reef. In light of our "fifth compartment" discussion, let's say a guy gets a social media friend request, or a text message or e-mail, from a woman. She may be an old high school flame, the girl at the office, whatever. They talk online. He starts to get a little too close for comfort as a result of the continuous banter back and forth with the woman.

Fail #2 - Captain Schettino has executed the same "too close to the reef" maneuver three or four times before without any backlash. In our social media case study, the man who has been chatting with the woman has actually talked to her three or four times before, and it's pretty harmless. Nothing really happens when they talk other than the conversations get a little more playful each time. Ultimately, they decide to get together real time (that's "in person" for you non-social media types). Before I continue, please burn this into your brain. There is rarely such thing as a "harmless lunch" with someone of the opposite sex. Even if nothing questionable is going on, what would your wife say? What would a friend who happens to see you at the coffee shop say? What would Jesus say? Let's move on…

Fail #3 - The ship's owner has made it clear that the maneuver was unauthorized and it was solely Captain Schettino's call. With regard to our "date," the man rationalizes in his mind that meeting the woman really isn't hurting anyone since his wife doesn't know anyway. Besides, when he's with the other woman, he feels like he's still got game. The more he hangs out with her, the better he feels about himself. She makes him feel good about himself, and his wife is really on him all the time. Over time, he may even convince himself he has fallen out of love with his wife and this woman is really the one for him. I'm not fabricating this, men. I've seen it time and time again.

Fail #4 - Captain Schettino jumps ship instead of rescuing his passengers. Similarly, our man decides that leaving his family for the new girl would be so much better for everybody. He rationalizes that the kids would be happier because he would be happier. The marriage slams into a reef, and the kids are left drowning, wondering why Daddy left. His wife begs for counseling and asks him to keep the family together. But he has already fallen into a lifeboat, so to speak, and he isn't turning back.

Fail #5 - Even when asked by the port officials to return to his ship, Captain Schettino declines to do so. And just like the ship's captain, our man simply declines reconciliation and counseling, breaks the family apart, and the collateral damage is far more devastating that an actual shipwreck.

Do you happen to know what the number one fear of the average child is? Obviously, it is the fear of a violent crime being committed against an immediate family member. But do you know what their second greatest fear is? That Mom and Dad don't stay together. Yet, in spite of this fear, men (and women) continue to flirt with marital disaster by getting way too close to people they should be steering clear of.

With the inception of social media, it has become increasingly likely for men and women to reconnect or, in some cases, meet for the first time. While Web-based dating sites are fast becoming the preferred way for people to meet, social media platforms have also created a dangerous "gray" area, and thousands of people cross into it every day. With a self-proclaimed 200 million users every day, is it any wonder the legal community also cites that one in five divorces are somehow related to social media like Facebook? That means that, statistically, 20%

of doomed marriages are saying social media was the culprit. And there are guys out there who have already flooded the first four compartments and are dangerously close to number five.

That being said, if you have found social media is pulling you in the wrong direction, try this: First, take an inventory of the women (or men, if you happen to be a woman) you have on your "Friends" or "Followers" list. Then ask yourself why they are on the list. Be honest with yourself, and immediately cut them from your friends if there is no good reason. While we can rationalize it all day long, God knows the motive, right?

> *Our purpose is to please God, not people. He alone examines the motives of our hearts.*
>
> 1 Thessalonians 2:4b (NLT)

After you've purged your "Friends" list of any questionable links, put a safety net in play. There are a number of ways you can protect yourself from the temptation of connecting with someone you shouldn't be talking to. In my discussions with men who have gotten in too deep in social media, the breach of conduct occurs when things aren't so good on the homefront. A simple argument with a spouse—or the cumulative results of feeling unwanted or underappreciated—can crack the door for Satan to get a cyber-foothold. The solution? Share your password with a guy you trust who can "lurk" (that means "spy" for you non-social media types) your page any time he wants to. He can even see your private messages.

You can take it a step further by sharing your password with your spouse. Remember, those who have nothing to hide, hide nothing, right? I have even seen a lot of Christian friends of mine opting for the combined couples page, where both the husband and the wife share the same profile. My wife and I, while maintaining separate profiles on several different social media platforms, have an arrangement when it comes to receiving "Friend Requests" from the opposite gender. Often, it is merely the spouse of someone one of us happens to already be friends with, but we just eliminate the redundancy by narrowing our friend base to the same sex only. If you were to bird dog my profile, you would find only female relatives (and a couple of teachers) in my 3,000-plus member friends list.

Simply put, we both have a boilerplate reply we send back to the requester that kindly declines the said request. While some may feel this is an extreme measure, it is wildly successful at both keeping our profiles free of potential challenges, and it is also a great witness. If you are so led, feel free to steal and reword my simple reply:

Hi [insert name here]:

I received your friend request and didn't want you to think I was ignoring you. My wife and I have a policy on [social media name] that we only accept friend requests from the same gender. I think you may already be her friend, but if not, please make sure you send her a request. Please understand that this is nothing personal but rather our way of guarding our marriage.

Blessings!

In my experiences thus far, people are cool with the reply. In fact, some are even very complimentary of the gender guard we have in play. I promise you won't miss the extra friends, and the peace of mind both for you and your wife is worth it.

Now comes the hard part. If you (or maybe you have "a friend" who), have gotten into dangerously shallow water and want to avert a potential major catastrophe, here are some urgent course corrections:

1. End it. Now. Take it from a guy who is divorced and remarried... the damage caused by a broken home is catastrophic and resonates for a very long time.

2. If you are even remotely considering leaving home, tell your wingman. Pray for a clean break with the "other woman." Have him hold you accountable. Often.

3. King David paid a steep price for his affair with Bathsheba. In 2 Samuel 12, the prophet Nathan drops the hammer on King David:

    Then Nathan said to David, "You are the man! This is what the Lord, the God of Israel, says: 'I anointed you king over Israel, and I delivered you from the hand of Saul. I gave your master's house to you, and your master's wives into your arms. I gave you the house of Israel and Judah. And if all this had been too little, I would have given you even more. Why did you despise the word of the Lord by doing what is evil in his eyes? You struck down Uriah the Hittite with the sword and took his wife to be your own. You killed him with the sword of the Ammonites. Now, therefore, the sword will never depart from your house, because you despised me and took the wife of Uriah the Hittite to be your own.'"

    2 Samuel 12:7-10

Don't be "the man."

1. Don't get cocky and think you're infallible. If you are going to back up another man in an effort to help him survive any form of infidelity, be on guard:

   ...If another believer is overcome by some sin, you who are godly should gently and humbly help that person back onto the right path. And be careful not to fall into the same temptation yourself.

   Galatians 6:1

2. Guard your eyes. Always. That "greener" grass on the other side of the fence is usually fertilized with cow manure.

   "I have made a covenant with my eyes not to look lustfully at a girl."

   Job 31:1

Jesus puts the lust of the eyes in proper perspective, and it not only applies to Internet pornography but also to social media connections:

"But I tell you that anyone who looks at a woman lustfully has already committed adultery with her in his heart."

Matthew 5:28

The captain of the *Titanic* was overconfident in his craft, and the captain of the *Costa Corcordia* made one simple course deviation that resulted in countless deaths. They both compromised, if only for a second.

Whenever we compromise, we set ourselves up for tragedy. I heard a funny story not too long ago of a 15-year-old young man who desperately wanted to see an R-rated movie. His mother was completely opposed to the idea and reminded him that he needed to be 17 and that R-rated movies were not good for him. He begged and pleaded.

"But it only has 'adult language,' 'adult humor,' and 'brief nudity,' Mom," he said. "It's only a little bad stuff."

His mother finally conceded, saying, "Okay. But I want to send some brownies with you and your friends. I'll make them while you get ready to go."

As the boy excitedly ran upstairs to get ready, his mother began mixing up a big batch of chocolate brownie mix. But before pouring them into the pan, she ducked outside and found a pile of their pet dog's "poop," scooped up a little piece, and blended it into the brownies.

The boy came charging downstairs, ready to see the movie, and upon seeing the brownies, he grabbed one. Just as he was about ready to bite into it, his mother shouted, "Wait! There's dog poop in those brownies." Then she said, "But only a little bit." By the way, if we have to validate our actions by using phrases like "it's just" or "it's only," then we have just red-flagged a potential compromise with our own words.

Even a little poop can kill the whole dessert. Doing life God's way while compromising even the slightest can ruin a good thing. We may think we have it all good, with the exception of something we don't really regard as all that big of a deal. I mean, after all, we have it 99% right. That's pretty good, isn't it? But, over time, even being just one degree off course can be a disaster.

In aviation, for every degree of you fly off course, you miss your landing spot by 92 feet for every mile that you fly. That's no big deal if you drive to the convenience store a mile up the street and you are one degree off heading. You might miss the parking lot or end up across the street. But if you were flying from Atlanta to Los Angeles, you would miss the airport by more than 40 miles. The longer we fly along with life, even a mere one degree off line from the will of God, the farther away we end up from where He wants us to land. The trick is to never compromise. Ever.

I don't know about you, but crashing into rocks is not on my bucket list, nor is missing the runway while flying cross-country. The idea of compromise is where the proverbial rubber meets the road when it comes to having another man in your life.

Whether you are already married, divorced, or have yet to get married, marriage is a battlefield where the enemy will stop at nothing to bring complete devastation. And Satan has found a very comfortable niche in social media, and he is using it to drive men into compromising what matters the most. Without a co-pilot to keep the flight on track or a helmsman to keep the ship aimed straight, we are setting ourselves up for potential disaster. So let's covenant with God and with each other to stay the course and finish the race set before us. In the words of Apollo 13 flight director, Gene Kranz, "failure is not an option."

Activation Questions

- *What safeguards do I have in place when it comes to the Internet, social media and chatrooms?*

- *Looking at all of the facets of my personal life, am I sailing with flooded compartments? How many?*

- *What could potentially be the tipping point that floods the fifth compartment and consequently sinks my entire ship? Who will drown with me? My family? My marriage?*

- *Do I need help surviving an attack on my integrity right now?*

22.

I DON'T KNOW WHAT HAPPENED TO ME
(When Guys Get Saved)

W e have spent quite a few chapters beating up on ourselves, so it's high time we read about something a little
more fun and a whole lot more exciting.

Sean Porter works at a juvenile detention facility in Los Angeles, California. As Porter quickly discovers, even while in-
carcerated the kids perpetuate their street gang battles. So he
decides to create a football program to encourage teamwork
and sportsmanship. Two young men, Willie Weathers from the
street gang "The 88's" and Kelvin Owens from the "95's" gang,
continue to brawl in spite of Porter's efforts to develop the young
men into football players. The chasm between these two gang
members, and the true story of Sean Porter, are both brilliantly
portrayed in the movie *The Gridiron Gang*, starring Dwayne
"The Rock" Johnson as Coach Porter and a cast of very talented
young actors-turned-gang members.

In spite of Porter's leadership, both Weathers and Owens
square off quite a few times in the movie. Outside of the fence,
the two men just happen to live a mere seven blocks from each
other (88th Street and 95th Street, as their gang names indicate),
and Sean Porter attempts to reconcile their differences in order to move the peace out of the prison and into the streets.
But both men, driven by the legacy of their respective street

gangs, refuse to turn their backs on their gangs, regardless of what Coach Porter attempts.

The relationship between Owens and Weathers ultimately takes a horrible turn when an outsider from Weathers' "88" street gang shoots the rival Owens in the shoulder after a football game. As the attacker is poised to shoot Owens a second time (this time in the head), Willie Weathers tackles his fellow gang member and saves Owens' life. The shooter looks at Weathers, completely stunned he would turn his back on his own gang to save a rival from the "95's," and is subsequently shot by police. Kelvin Owens survives, and Weathers struggles to determine why he violated a vital gang rule to save another man's life. As Willie sits in an isolation cell, Coach Porter comes in to reinforce that the gang member has indeed changed.

Porter: You go back to the 'hood, they're gonna put a bullet in your head. They think you're not down for the set any more, no matter what you say now. You know what? I think they're right!

[Willie jumps up and attacks Porter, screaming profanities at him]

Porter: *[deflecting Willie's punches]* I'm all you got. Who else cares about you?!

Willie: I don't need nobody else!

Porter: You don't give a [expletive deleted] about me or anybody else!

Willie: Man, that's right!

Porter: Then why'd you try and save Kelvin yesterday? Huh? Answer me that! Why'd you side with the enemy over your own homeboy?

Willie: 'Cuz of you! And this football team, man!

[Willie bursts into tears]

Porter: You made a choice!

Willie: *[sobbing]* No, I didn't! I didn't even know what was happening to me. It was just so... everything was so quick. I don't even know what's happening to me, man.

Porter: I do. You're not the loser you were when you first got here, Willie.

The Gridiron Gang movie has such a poignant tagline. It simply reads: *"One goal. A second chance."* In the Bible, that tagline would read:

> *Therefore, if anyone is in Christ, he is a new creation; the old has gone, the new has come!*
>
> 2 Corinthians 5:17

Personally, I like the way the New Living Translation states the same verse:

> *This means that anyone who belongs to Christ has become a new person. The old life is gone; a new life has begun!*
>
> 2 Corinthians 5:17 (NLT)

The tale of Willie Weathers isn't too different from a lot of men we meet. Maybe Willie is even just like us, as I know his character is a lot like me. Before Christ, we live a life all for us until the day we are finally broken and cry out to God. In a fleeting moment, when the Holy Spirit moves in, we realize we are no longer the same guy. We are changed from the inside out.

Regardless of how old or young we are, when guys like us decide to turn our shattered lives over to the Lordship of Jesus Christ, a couple of really crazy phenomena happen. The first one you just read about is where we respond completely differently than our previous "self." Instead of self-absorbed combatants, we become compassionate peacekeepers.

As I have shared already, you know I have a past life, which in my case spanned nearly 30 years. Let's call him "Dave." Dave's life was filled with a lot of alcohol, drug induced stupors, broken relationships and a cynical anger that could rob anyone's joy in mere seconds. The people who still remember "Dave" likely recall a hard-partying pathological liar with a brutally sarcastic edge and no love for anyone or anything. Incessantly negative, always brash and just plain rude, Dave was awful. There are literally hundreds of people who only know him and not the new creation, known as "David," who came into being on a fateful day after losing absolutely everything that mattered and everything that didn't. Crushed and hopeless, "David" was birthed from the pain of loss and crisis. "David" is kind, compassionate, loving and full of hope; "Dave" is dead.

The second supernatural transformation occurs with regard to our passion for Jesus. In short, we want to tell everyone we know about Him and what He did for us. Today! Remember being an evangelistic superfreak? I couldn't even go to the store without sharing Jesus, but over time my zeal sort of faded. Even today, I am certain that it isn't that I've lost my fire for the Lord. I think it may just be due to the repeated rejection as I tried to evangelize the world.

I recall a time of major medical crisis in the life of one of my friends, and I had flown in to visit him. His son was very sick, and my friend only knew "Dave." In fact, since moving away from my friends, this was my first visit as a "new creation."

While I was met with some skepticism based on just how horrible "Dave" was, I was determined to let both Jesus and the new "David" shine through. I looked for people at the children's hospital to pray with and made bold invitations to know Jesus. Since I know He often uses crisis moments to reach men, I was going to be bold. But nothing seemed to happen after the prayers were over. To this day, there is a scene in *Jerry Maguire* that reminds me so much of this time in my life.

Jerry is a sports agent in Los Angeles, working for one of the biggest sports agencies in the nation. His company represents virtually every major sports star, and Jerry is just as cutthroat as his colleagues. The sports business is brutal, centered on nothing more than money and possessing few, if any, ethics. When confronted by the child of a professional athlete who has again suffered a concussion, Jerry decides it's time to bring the heart back into the sports agency game. He drafts a lengthy plan to forego big money and instead cultivate loving relationships, and he is summarily run out of the agency. As Jerry packs up his office, he walks into a large "boiler room" full of desks and ringing phones and begins a powerful monologue:

Jerry: Well... don't worry. I'm not gonna do what you all think I'm gonna do, which is just flip out.

[He flails like an insane man]

Let me just say, as I ease out of the office I helped build, I'm sorry, but it's a fact that there's such a thing as manners. A way of treating people.

[He points at the office aquarium]

These fish have manners. In fact, I'm starting a new company and the fish will come with me. Call me sentimental, but the fish are coming with me. Okay. If anybody else wants to come with me, this is a chance for something real and fun and inspiring in this godforsaken business, and we will do it together.

[He invites people with his hands]

Who's coming with me? Who's coming with me? Who's coming with me besides… Flipper here?

[No one moves in the office]

This is embarrassing. All right.

[Turns to his secretary]

Wendy, shall we?

Wendy: Ah Jer, I'm three months away from the pay increase…

Jerry ends up completely dejected and rejected by absolutely everyone in the office. In fact, only one person ends up following him.

Have you ever walked into a room full of people you just KNOW need Jesus, and you bring Him into the room, make an incredible presentation of the gospel, and then say like Jerry: "Who's coming with me? Who's coming with me?" You can almost hear the crickets chirp sometimes, right? And, over time, the passion to spread the Word sort of dies out.

It's surprising, but Jesus Himself not only speaks of this issue but also actually experiences it Himself. In Jesus' parable of the great banquet, we read of the trouble a man has just getting guests to show up for dinner:

> *"A certain man was preparing a great banquet and invited many guests. At the time of the banquet he sent his servant to tell those who had been invited, 'Come, for everything is now ready.' But they all alike began to make excuses. The first said, 'I have just bought a field, and I must go and see it. Please*

excuse me.' Another said, 'I have just bought five yoke of oxen, and I'm on my way to try them out. Please excuse me.' Still another said, 'I just got married, so I can't come.'"

Luke 14:16-20

Of course, Jesus was talking about the ultimate invitation to become a part of the kingdom of heaven through accepting His death and His invitation to be with Him. And we will encounter people who just aren't ready to make that decision yet. Just like Jerry Maguire's secretary, who wouldn't leave the agency because of her upcoming pay increase, the people invited in the parable all make lame excuses. The above dialogue goes on to say that "many are called, but few are chosen," so don't take it personally if you get rejected. Even Jesus Himself got hit with a lame excuse after inviting a man to follow Him:

Now a man came up to Jesus and asked, "Teacher, what good thing must I do to get eternal life?"

"Why do you ask me about what is good?" Jesus replied. "There is only One who is good. If you want to enter life, obey the commandments."

"Which ones?" the man inquired.

Jesus replied, "'Do not murder, do not commit adultery, do not steal, do not give false testimony, honor your father and mother,' and 'love your neighbor as yourself.'"

"All these I have kept," the young man said. "What do I still lack?"

Jesus answered, "If you want to be perfect, go, sell your possessions and give to the poor, and you will have treasure in heaven. Then come, follow me."

When the young man heard this, he went away sad, because he had great wealth.

Matthew 19:16-22

Men, no matter how many weak excuses you hear, just keep asking. Our mission is to stand men before the door and ask them to knock. I used to work with a guy who, even when faced with a potentially bad medical diagnosis, simply refused to accept Jesus. "I'll get around to it," he would say, "but I'm not ready to give up my 'Texas Hold 'Em' habit yet."

The way I figure it, a major league baseball player hitting .300 is having a stellar season. In simple math, that is 30%. That means seven out of every 10 times at bat he is NOT hitting the ball. It's not the number of times we connect with the ball but the number of at-bats that really matters. If we just give up trying to reach out to our friends because they remember the "old us" or, worse yet, come up with some weak excuse, we are missing one of our major roles in God's army: recruiting.

Your own personal testimony, failures and all, may be the ONLY thing that will bring the people in your sphere of influence to Jesus. Your life is perfectly designed to reach the people God places in your path. So instead of backing up, let's press in and relentlessly pursue others for the Lord. If we don't do it, who will?

Activation Questions

- *Have I ever had a time where I didn't recognize my own response? A time where I first noticed the Holy Spirit had changed me?*

- *Have I ever made the effort to tell my friends about what Jesus did for me? Why not?*

- *Who can I reach out to right now to tell about God?*

23

THAT IS WHY YOU FAIL
(Pray Like a Man)

"God isn't listening to me," my buddy said. "I pray and pray and nothing happens." I can't count the number of times I have heard men say this. Actually, I can't count the number of times I have said it. We have been programmed to pray, but to be honest, it's a weak, underwhelming attempt at talking to God. As frustrations mount, we try different words. "Well, the conversation style of prayer didn't work, so I guess I'll shift into King James language." When that doesn't work, we add more Scripture. And when that prayer still doesn't get answered, we even start trying different combinations of people. "The Bible says where two or more are gathered, and Steve and Bill didn't work. Think I'll try John and Jim. Maybe God will listen to them."

Hey! That's not the problem! I could just tell you, but since I love using movies as illustrations, I'm going to lay this one down "Yoda" style.

In *Star Wars* circles, *The Empire Strikes Back* is titled *Episode V*. We old guys know it's really episode two, as the ones that came after will never be as good as the first three. I was 12 years old in 1977, when THE *Star Wars* movie came out. No, it wasn't called *A New Hope*, bro. It was just *Star Wars*

When *Star Wars* came out, there was also no such thing as videotapes, pay-per-view, or DVDs, so if you wanted to see the movie, you had to go to the theater. This movie had a first run that lasted almost a year and grossed more than $461 million on its first pass through theaters. Since it was a huge hit for a kid like me, I would be willing to bet I contributed at least half of that... not really, but it sure seemed like it. I remember one summer in the 1970s where, as usual, my parents went on a cruise and left my sister and me with our grandparents in Hollywood, Florida. And every day I would beg my grandmother to take us to see *Star Wars*. And like any good grandmother, she did, but only after a pit stop at Burger King, where I would get a Double Whopper with cheese. Needless to say, I was fat and I was happy!

If you remember the plot of the first installment, Luke Skywalker has lost his uncle and aunt and has become friends with Obi-Wan Kenobi. You may also recall Obi-Wan is killed by Darth Vader in a lightsaber duel near the end of *Star Wars*, only his body is never recovered. Obi-Wan is just sort of raptured out of his robes. From this point in the *Star Wars* trilogy, Ben Kenobi becomes a Force ghost, occasionally interacting with his favorite kid, Luke. Luke's dream is to be a Jedi, and when we rejoin Luke, Leia, Han Solo, and the rest of the crew in *The Empire Strikes Back*, Luke is well on his way to becoming a Jedi Knight.

The Rebel base has been relocated to the ice planet of Hoth, and Luke and Han embark on their Tauntauns (my guess is you'll never see that word in another Christian men's book) to investigate some strange asteroids landing on the planet. Luke and Han end up separated, with Han returning to the Rebel base while Luke is attacked by the Wampa, a creature that actually resembles the Abominable Snowman from *Rudolph the*

Red-Nosed Reindeer. Luke escapes but nearly freezes to death in the snow after his Tauntaun dies.

Unable to allow Luke to die in the cold, Han himself risks freezing to death and goes hunting for Luke. Meanwhile, Luke, delirious from the cold, looks up to see the ever-present Obi-Wan Force ghost. "You will go to the Dagobah system. There you will learn from Yoda, the Jedi Master who instructed me." Just as Obi-Wan finishes his orders, Han arrives and Luke is saved. And Luke sets his sights on Dagobah.

Now, at this point, I would imagine Luke has envisioned Yoda in his mind. He is a Jedi Master, after all, so he must be seven feet tall and virtually indestructible. Upon crash landing his X-wing fighter on the swamp planet of Dagobah, Luke quickly realizes Yoda is actually three feet tall, green, has pointy ears, and sounds surprisingly like Fozzie Bear from the Muppets (both were voiced by Frank Oz and sound the same).

Our scene commences in the middle of Luke's training, and he performs a handstand with Yoda on his feet as Luke stacks rocks with his mind. I know; it's science fiction. And right in the middle of stacking the final rock, the little robot R2-D2 lets out a digital scream as Luke's partially submerged fighter begins to sink into the quagmire.

Luke: We'll never get it out now.

Yoda: So certain, are you? Always with you it cannot be done.

Luke: Master, moving rocks is one thing. But this is totally different!

Yoda: No! No different! Only different in your mind. You must unlearn what you have learned.

Luke: All right, I'll give it a try.

Yoda: No! Try not. Do or do not. There is no try.

After making a real effort to use his mind to rescue the ship from the water, Luke gives up and the ship ultimately sinks. Yoda then proceeds to tell Luke more about the Force, the supernatural power given to all Jedi knights. He speaks of his size being irrelevant in the economy of the Force and shares with the young Jedi trainee that Luke himself is not a physical being but rather a spiritual one. But even after all of the input, and like a lot of guys I know, Luke just disregards what the master is saying and dejectedly heads off into the woods to pout.

"You want the impossible," Luke mumbles as he walks away.

Then, as Luke sits in the woods, Yoda closes his eyes, raises a little green hand, and singlehandedly levitates the ship out of the swamp and onto the adjacent beach. As Luke walks around the now dry ship, he says, "I... I don't believe it!"

Yoda simply replies with, "That is why you fail."

In light of prayer, let the phrase "that is why you fail" resonate for a minute. Maybe, just maybe, it isn't the language, format, or people we solicit to pray with us. Could it be our level of faith? Remember what Jesus said to His disciples:

> *"I tell you the truth, if you have faith as small as a mustard seed, you can say to this mountain, 'Move from here to there' and it will move. Nothing will be impossible for you."*
>
> *Matthew 17:20*

I have to pause here for a second, guys, because I spent two decades living in Portland, Oregon, a city with 11,250-foot Mount Hood shadowing the city to the east. I spent a lot of time skiing on that mountain, and even on my best "faith" day I have a hard time envisioning telling Mt. Hood to move. So I promise you I am convicting my lack of faith, and you are just sort of going along for the ride.

In light of this and Yoda's dialogue with young Luke, let's unpack a few choice quotes from the movie and see how this may apply to our relative lack of faith.

Right out of the gate, Luke says, "We'll never get it out now." Can I make a suggestion? Since we already know the power of words can bless or curse a situation, why not choose to eradicate the word "never" from our vocabulary? I hear people use this word all the time. "This is never going to work out" or "I'm never going to get my life right." Instead of opening the door to failure, why not bless the situation with a more positive affirmation instead?

Like many of us faced with a seemingly impossible task, Luke goes on to say, "Master, moving rocks is one thing. This is totally different."

Think about this for a minute. How often do we do exactly the same thing to God? "God can certainly heal my marriage," we think, "but there is no way He can help me pay the mortgage. I'm eight months behind." Really? If God owns the cattle on a thousand hills (see Psalm 50:10), then our little mortgage is nothing to the Creator. Nothing is impossible with God, or so we say. But why don't we actually believe it?

Then Yoda fires back, "No! No different! Only different in your mind. You must unlearn what you have learned."

Whenever I hear our little green friend utter those words, I'm immediately led to a very specific Scripture that almost says the same thing:

*Do not conform any longer to the pattern of this world, but
be transformed by the renewing of your mind.*

Romans 12:2a

Even when it comes to faith and prayer, we must forget what
the world tells us. The ship isn't too big, and the mortgage isn't
too expensive. As a disclaimer, please understand I don't put too
much credence in prosperity doctrine. I truly don't buy into the
fact God wants all of us to have a Ferrari or a big house. In fact,
did you happen to see the movie *Bruce Almighty*? It's about a
man who is given the responsibility of "being God" in order to
understand God. And to make his life really easy, Bruce just answers all of the prayers with "yes." A few million people end up
winning the lottery one night, and they each get about $1.26.
God will indeed check our motives and say "no" if it isn't His
will for us. And in light of the concept of assuming God wants
us all to live a life of comfort, take a good hard look at the disciples and the way they died. Somehow, I just don't think being
stoned to death, cut in half, or hung upside down on a cross is
too prosperous.

Back to Luke, he finally just quits and walks away. "You want
the impossible" is all he manages to say, as he flops down on the
ground to pout. But guess what?

For nothing is impossible with God

Luke 1:37

So what's the problem now? If you're like me, maybe you just
figure God isn't listening because of the way you live. I used to
hang my hat on what James said:

The effectual fervent prayer of a righteous man availeth much

James 5:16 (KJV)

I'm not exactly sure why I only know that Scripture in the King James Version. I guess I just memorized it that way. Once you cut through the 1611 jargon, I believe it simply says the continuous prayers of a righteous man are effective. In other words, a righteous guy can pray and see a lot of stuff happen, right?

That, my brothers, is where I immediately disqualify myself. I live in Southwest Florida, the home of the worst drivers on the planet. We're talking "right turn out of the far left lane" or "drive 27 MPH on the freeway" bad drivers. And consequently, I tend to get very unrighteous in the way I handle some of their wild vehicular maneuvers. To put it bluntly, I am not righteous in any way, shape, or form. And since James says I need to be in order to be an effective prayer guy, I just stop praying altogether.

Here's some good news. None of us are righteous. We are only made righteous by the blood shed on the cross at Calvary. Through His death, we are made righteous. And on top of that, on more than one occasion, the Bible cites Abraham as believing God. And in so doing, it was credited to him as righteousness! So through the shed blood of Jesus and a belief in God's plan for us, we can indeed be the righteous praying man to whom James alludes. We just need to claim it and pray.

Even knowing all of this myself, prayer is without a doubt one of the most difficult things for me to do. I have months where I am like Daniel in the Bible, diligently praying three times every day for everything in my life. There are months where I get up at 5 a.m. to pray before the family gets up. But in between those fleeting moments of spiritual superstardom are long prayer droughts. I go from a prayer warrior to a meek guy who can barely muster a dinner prayer like the following: "We thank You, God, for peas and meat. We thank you God for good things to eat." Sure, I can read the Word like a beast, but my prayer life tanks pretty often.

After looking into my own prayer life and talking to men all over the country, I have discovered something: Even though we often appear to be the masters of our own universe, we pray like we don't expect anything to ever happen. Let me illustrate what I mean by backing up to the first generation of Christian men.

In Chapter 3 of the Book of Acts, Peter and John heal a beggar who was crippled from birth. As the stunned onlookers stand around, Peter begins to preach the name of Jesus. By the time we get into Acts 4, Peter and John are treading on thin ice with the local government:

> *The priests and the captain of the temple guard and the Sadducees came up to Peter and John while they were speaking to the people. They were greatly disturbed because the apostles were teaching the people and proclaiming in Jesus the resurrection of the dead. They seized Peter and John, and because it was evening, they put them in jail until the next day.*
>
> *Acts 4:1-3*

Peter and John get some overnight accommodations in jail, and then they get the added pleasure of a reprimand from the local government (aka, "The Sanhedrin") the next morning. In a nutshell, the men are strongly cautioned to cease and desist from preaching the name of Jesus in the streets of their fair city.

During the proceedings, Peter gets up and tells the Sanhedrin about Jesus. And, after firing a lot of empty threats at Peter and John, the Sanhedrin lets them leave. The Bible goes on to recount the trip home:

> *On their release, Peter and John went back to their own people and reported all that the chief priests and elders had said to them.*
>
> *Acts 4:23*

In other words, Peter and John tell all of their fellow Jesus followers they can no longer preach in the streets

> *When they heard this, they raised their voices together in prayer to God. "Sovereign Lord," they said, "you made the heaven and the earth and the sea, and everything in them. You spoke by the Holy Spirit through the mouth of your servant, our father David: 'Why do the nations rage and the peoples plot in vain? The kings of the earth take their stand and the rulers gather together against the Lord and against his Anointed One.'"*
>
> *Acts 4:24-26*

And during their prayer, they add a few requests:

> *Now, Lord, consider their threats and enable your servants to speak your word with great boldness. Stretch out your hand to heal and perform miraculous signs and wonders through the name of your holy servant Jesus*
>
> *Acts 4:29-30*

Let's move that story into the present day for a minute. I live in the Tampa Bay area, so I am going to simply use my own area to paint a picture. It's Sunday, and the Tampa Bay Buccaneers (the local NFL team) are set to lose again this weekend at Raymond James Stadium (their home field). I have decided a buddy and I are going to go to the stadium early to hand out Bible tracts and share the Word with the attendees before the game. Within a few minutes, the police approach us and tell us to stop passing out Bible stuff. Since they are offended and it's almost kick-off, they decide to toss my friend and I into the county jail until Monday morning.

After a brief appearance before the judge, and after receiving a firm warning to discontinue religious activities at the stadium, my friend and I are set free.

Now, like most men who have had their rights violated, I return home livid. These people had thrown me in jail for absolutely nothing and had violated my First Amendment rights to free speech. So I gather my board of directors and we formulate a game plan to sue the NFL, the City of Tampa and even Raymond James, whose name is on the stadium. The lawyers immediately set things in motion, bent on taking this case all the way to the Supreme Court.

Another guy calls the media. We get all of the major networks involved and even call Nancy Grace and Geraldo to try and get as much coverage as possible. After all, this is the story of men who were wrongfully imprisoned. We also connect with all of the newspapers and hope to get picked up by the wire services so the story goes international.

But, because of the nature of the event, we get disregarded. No one cares that two Christian men were jailed for nothing, so the media slowly drops us. Similarly, the court system fails to award us the millions of dollars in damages we are seeking, and even the Supreme Court ultimately sends us down the road empty-handed.

So we all get back together, feeling thoroughly defeated, when one of our friends makes this statement: "Well. We've done all we can. I guess all we can do now is pray."

In light of the first Christians, let's look at one part of Acts 4 again:

"When they heard this, they raised their voices together in prayer to God."

Notice that nowhere in Acts 4 do they hire an attorney or search out the local scribe. The first thing these disciples do is pray. The second they hear of Peter's plight, they hit their knees.

Every day, I hear from men in deep financial turmoil. Some are in deep with the mortgage lenders and are mere months from foreclosure. The dialogue is always similar, with the men telling me about the relatives from whom they've borrowed, the concessions they've made by cancelling cable, and how they eating Ramen noodles and bike to work. They tell of countless letters to the bank and failed attempts to re-structure the loan. And with loss looming on the horizon, they reach out and say, "I've done all I can financially. All I can do now is pray about this."

Why is it that Christian men today immediately jump into "fix-it" mode before we call on the Creator of the universe? When did we decide to start using prayer as a last resort instead of as a front line attack on the problem? As if we can somehow do it better than the Lord can, and as if our limited resources are somehow suitable for seemingly unwinnable circumstances.

Here's a supernatural paradigm shift, gentlemen. If it's big enough to lose sleep over and big enough to consume your thoughts every waking minute of every day, how about calling on the Almighty to step into the ring on your behalf? Let Him fight the battle for you!

And don't let doubt jam up the works. If doubt does thwart the efficiency of prayer, it's really okay. Just don't let it counteract your faith. I suffer from a world-class case of spiritual amnesia sometimes. Since I am such a movie buff, I tell guys there are days when I feel like Jason Bourne with a Bible (for those of you who don't know who Jason Bourne is, he's a special agent who gets amnesia and spends three whole movies trying to figure out who he is). I am a big doubter sometimes, and I always take great solace in knowing I follow some pretty big "doubter" footsteps.

Let me tell you a story of 12 men who were hanging out with Jesus as He heard of the untimely death of His friend, John the Baptist. When He heard of John's beheading, He took off, but droves of people followed Him. Check out what happens next:

> *As evening approached, the disciples came to him and said, "This is a remote place, and it's already getting late. Send the crowds away, so they can go to the villages and buy themselves some food."*
>
> *Matthew 14:15*

If you have spent a minute in Sunday School, you know Jesus took five little loaves of bread and two fish, gave thanks to God, broke the bread, and had the disciples pass the food out to 5,000 men. The men ate until they were full, and the disciples ended up picking up 12 baskets of leftovers, ironically (or was it?) the precise number of disciples.

Now I don't know how you feel about this, but these disciples saw what can only be classified as a food miracle. Remember also that they had seen Jesus raise people from the dead, heal the terminally ill, and give sight to the blind. They were right there in the same room with Jesus, so you would think they would be completely sold on the idea He was indeed God in the flesh. At one point, Peter even declares that Jesus is indeed the Messiah. Think your faith armor is chinked? Don't feel bad, and check this out:

Some time after He fed 5,000 men, Jesus is sitting on a hillside along with 4,000 of His closest friends. It's getting late.

> *Jesus called his disciples to him and said, "I have compassion for these people; they have already been with me three days and have nothing to eat. I do not want to send them away hungry, or they may collapse on the way." His disciples answered, "Where could we get enough bread in this remote place to feed such a crowd?"*
>
> *Matthew 15:32-33*

Did the disciples seriously just say what I think they said? Don't they remember what Jesus did when the 5,000 men were hungry? This was a thousand fewer men, and the disciples really had no idea where they would get food?

This time, Jesus takes seven loaves of bread and a few fish, and seven baskets of leftovers remained after all had eaten. Seven, by the way, is the biblical number of perfection... also no accident, I would imagine.

The disciples saw Jesus work firsthand, yet the Bible says:

"...Blessed are those who have not seen and yet have believed."

John 20:29b

And that is the category we fit into, men. So it's time to shake off the doubt and call on the Creator to stand in the gap for us during our greatest time of need. I would encourage you to take a few minutes and create what I like to call an "Ephesians 3:20" list. The Scripture I am referencing says:

Now to him who is able to do immeasurably more than all we ask or imagine, according to his power that is at work within us

Ephesians 3:20

Read it again. It clearly says He can do more than we can ask or imagine. I don't know about you, but I can imagine an awful lot. And the Word says that God can blow that away. So make a list of the most absurd prayer requests you have on your heart and begin to pray incessantly about them. Remember to gauge your motives, as God certainly will.

If you had all of the resources in the kingdom at your disposal, what would you pray for? Write them down. Don't get stuck in the here and now, and skip the little logistics like money or time since God does.

Our first 3:20 list contained some pretty over the top requests. When Joni and I did them separately, we discovered a small issue with our even smaller thinking. One prayer was to speak at Hillsong Church in Sydney, Australia, but before we even got down to praying, a couple of problems emerged. My wife pointed out that I didn't know the pastor, we didn't have the money to fly to Australia, and we had no idea what to do with our kids should we happen to go "Down Under." We both missed the point of the exercise. No limits. I am happy to say that God has tackled more than half of our first list thanks to a lot of prayer and our willingness to attack when the trumpet sounds.

As a final caution prior to embarking on the task at hand, remember God answers prayers in three ways. There are quite a few sermons on this, but this is what I have seen happen in my own life.

The first answer is "yes." There is no mistaking "yes." It just happens.

The second answer is "not yet." This requires that often missed fruit of the Spirit spirit called "patience." I actually prefer the word used in the King James translation of the Bible: "long-suffering." Basically, we have to suffer for a really long time! We simply aren't ready yet. But He will handle it in His time, not ours. So be relentless. It would be pretty pathetic if I gave up praying the day before God moved. What if Joshua had stopped praying for the wall of Jericho to fall down on the sixth day? The seventh day, and the subsequent walls falling, may have never happened. And if the door slams shut in your face, there's your final answer.

The last possible answer is the one we most often mistake for "no." It is simply "I have something better in mind." He is indeed going to handle the request but in a way that has no resemblance to how we think He will answer it. After years of praying for more time with my kids, God answered the prayer in a way I would have never suspected. So don't limit an infinite God with finite thoughts.

It is critical you share your prayer with your wingman. Commit to each other to praying until something happens. Be diligent in prayer for both you and for him.

Yoke yourself to another guy. His mission is to support, encourage, and even rebuke you. The Bible says, "Pity the man who falls and has no one to pick him up." Don't become a casualty. Find your cover fire and let's go to war.

Activation Questions

- *What is my greatest prayer request right now?*

- *Do I really believe that God is as big as I say He is?*

- *Who am I praying in agreement with about my request?*

- *When will my Ephesians 3:20 list be ready and who will help me pray them into reality?*